INSTALLING SUNROOFS & T-TOPS

CARL CAIATI

TAB BOOKS Inc.
Blue Ridge Summit, PA 17214

Other TAB Books by the Author

No. 1555   *Airbrushing*
No. 1955   *Advanced Airbrushing Techniques Made Simple*
No. 2112   *Customizing Your Van—2nd Edition (with Allan Girdler)*
No. 2122   *Basic Body Repair & Refinishing for the Weekend Mechanic*

FIRST EDITION

FIRST PRINTING

Library of Congress Cataloging in Publication Data

Caiati, Carl.
    Installing sunroofs and T-tops.

    Includes index.
    1. Automobiles—Sunroofs. I. Title.
TL275.C33   1985   629.2′6   85-4638
ISBN 0-8306-2132-6 (pbk.)

Front cover photographs:
        Mustang with Cars & Concepts T-top
        Courtesy: Cars & Concepts.
        Sunroof photograph courtesy of Hollandia.

Contents

Acknowledgments

Working on a new book involves much research and the assistance of many people and other sources.

I am particularly indebted to Martin Pot of Hollandia Sunroofs. Martin made a most concentrated effort in obtaining valuable photographs, historical and technical data on electric sunroofs, and other materials for me.

Phil Saladin of Cars & Concepts likewise helped, as did Bob Richards and Ernie Bunnell of Pacific, in forwarding valuable T-top material.

Alan Lewis has always come through with valuable material parts, and he provided assistance pertaining to pop-in sunroofs.

I would also like to thank the various product manufacturers in the sunroof and T-top field who provided product photos.

The T-top, a modern sports concept.

Introduction

In the 40- to 50-year period since its conception, the sunroof and T-top have gained a foothold with sports car and custom car buffs. The popularity of these (original equipment models), OEM or added luxury components is evidenced through their steadily growing acceptance by automotive manufacturers, dealers, and the consumer public alike.

Many of the sportier automotive offerings of today have sunroofs. The majority are the simple pop-in type with a removable glass panel. The more sophisticated luxury sedans usually opt for the state-of-the-art electric sunroofs, such as those manufactured by Hollandia of the Netherlands. Sunroof excellence is exhibited in such cars as the Volvo sedan luxury 400 series, the Jaguar "Saloon," Rolls-Royce, production Fiats, Datsun, and a host of others. Figure I-1 shows the 1983 Nissan Pulsar that includes a pop-in sunroof unit as an integral part of the roof structure. Figure I-2 shows the roof in its open position. The glass panel section is fully removable if desired, allowing for maximum ventilation.

For the car that does not contain a sunroof, there are a variety of fine aftermarket accessory sunroofs from which to choose. Many can be installed by the owner who is trained in metal cutting and the use of metal cutting tools, such as a saber saw, nibbler, or air chisel. Due to their worldwide acceptance and popularity, however, sunroofs can be installed by body-shop and automotive-service chains. Ziebart, the nationwide rustproofing establishment, now of-

Fig. I-1. Nissan Pulsar, sunroof version.

fers sunroof installation featuring products of accepted sunroof manufacturers.

The reasons for the surge in sunroof popularity are multiple but simple. Structurally, a sunroof improves the rigidity of the car roof. It can be a fast and convenient way to exit the car in an emergency, especially if the doors are blocked or jammed shut. The sunroof, open or closed, admits a considerable amount of sunlight. On hot summer days an open sunroof allows the car to cool quickly and efficiently. It provides continued, improved air flow all year round. Even the addition of the most basic sunroof offers air-

Fig. I-2. Close up of the Pulsar sunroof OEM feature.

conditioning much less expensive than standard mechanical systems.

Aftermarket accessory sunroofs come in many shapes suitable for mounting in all vehicles, provided you take the conforming roof size and area into consideration. The proper selection of a sunroof also enhances interior looks and styling (Fig. I-3) for a chosen vehicle.

A very novel sunroof like setup is the T-top. A *T-top* has two

Fig. I-3. Interior view of the Ford Bronco with accessory aftermarket sunroof.

Fig. I-4. A 1973 Chevy Corvette—T-top version. Courtesy Chevrolet.

x

pieces mounted separately on a common roof frame to become a structural part of the car's roof. According to Cars and Concepts, today's most respected T-top manufacturer, the first T-top was developed on paper in 1942. No hard prototype was produced, however, at that time.

The first company to act upon production of the T-top was Chevrolet in 1968. The first vehicle to benefit from the highly stylist T-top treatment was the Corvette. This helped make the T-top an accepted design. It also filled the gap for convertible buffs who enjoyed the fresh-air features of discontinued convertible models. Figure I-4 shows one of the very popular Corvette T-top versions.

With the request for T-topped cars multiplying, GM then offered T-top factory options for the Camaro and Firebird. T-top installations enhanced both the design and functions of these models. Figure I-5 shows an earlier Camaro T-top version; Fig. I-6 shows the 1980 Camaro. The addition of the T-tops in no way altered the already accepted sporty lines of the car while adding a custom touch. Today the T-top continues to be a desired factory option of the Camaro (Fig. I-7), Firebird, and the Corvette.

In 1976, Car & Concepts offered the first aftermarket T-tops while obtaining manufacturer and dealer contracts. The year before, on a special production basis, the first Hurst/Olds models were

Fig. I-5. A 1979 Camaro. Courtesy Chevrolet.

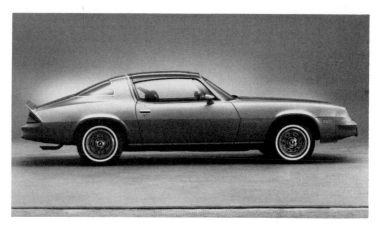

Fig. I-6. A 1983 Chevy Camaro. Courtesy Chevrolet.

marketed—2,535 were produced, all with T-roof options. Subsequently, conversions were offered on the Pontiac Firebird, Chevy Camaro, Pontiac Grand Prix, Chevrolet Monte Carlo, Oldsmobile Cutlass, Buick Regal, Dodge Aspen, and Plymouth Volare. Today, thanks to the enterprising efforts of sunroof and T-top manufacturers, a wide array of these desirable accessory items are available.

The T-top, a modern sports concept.

Chapter 1

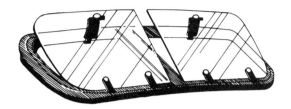

Types of Sunroofs and T-tops

Sunroofs, moon roofs, and T-tops share certain characteristics, though each is a bit different. The sunroofs (single panel and double panel types), moon roofs, and sophisticated electric sunroof have a single glass panel structure in common that mounts in a frame forming the complete unit. The T-top is also designed for letting more light and air into the vehicle. It becomes more of a structural part of the car or car roof, however, as the housing that contains each side or T-top panel when installed becomes a permanent part and cannot be removed. Except for damage due to accidents, the T-top becomes a permanent structural component. The sunroof is also a more or less permanent additive, but it can be replaced with a bigger or more sophisticated unit if so desired in the future.

For example, let's say you put a simple 15-×-30-inch sunroof in a Camaro and later decide that you want a larger electric sunroof in its place. All you need do is remove the old sunroof, enlarge the hole or opening to the appropriate size, and insert an entire electric sunroof unit. If, however, the identical type of car is outfitted for a T-top, and you want to switch to an electric unit or one piece sunroof, you are out of luck because the T-top roof modification is too radical and permanent (in comparison to a sunroof installation cutout). A roof can never again properly reconform after having undergone the radical surgery T-top installation involves.

SUNROOFS

With intensive research, the sunroof can be traced back to the horse and enclosed-buggy days. Openings were then provided in coach roofs for added ventilation, upgrading interior lighting, and for communicating with a coachman or driver. In automobiles, sunroofs similar to today's versions were introduced and used in Europe in the early 1930s by rich automobile clientele who owned and drove American cars such as Fords and Chevrolets.

The earliest known mass producer of the first sunroof was Vermeulen-Hollandia B.V. of the Netherlands. This company custom-fitted handmade units for installation in specific cars. Shortly after World War II, Hollandia developed the kit-form insertable sunroof. This early version included a canvas top. Later, in the early 1950s, the steel-panel-top sunroof was developed. To this day, Hollandia continues to market and upgrade the sunroof designs they originally produced.

The sunroof is probably the most popular and salable type of roof accessory. One-piece sunroofs range in size from the compact 15″ × 30″ to the small 17″ × 35″ to the large 20″ × 34″. A 16″ × 20″ specialized sunroof is also manufactured and used almost exclusively for the Volkswagen Beetle or Karman-Ghia.

The 15″ × 30″ size sunroof is ideal for smaller compacts like the Honda, Fiat, sports models, and other foreign miniversions. Virtually all in-between compacts, such as Datsun, Mazda, and Toyota,

Fig. 1-1. A simple one-piece, pop-up roof in an early Camaro roof.

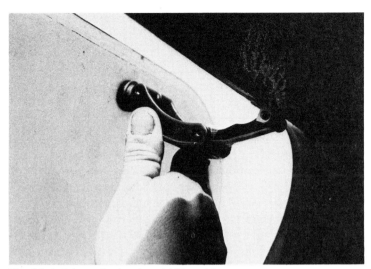
Fig. 1-2. Latch mechanism in a fold-type hinge.

can accommodate sunroofs up to 17″ × 35″ with no danger of the roof buckling or other damage when the sunroof unit is secured firmly. Larger sizes up to 20 × 34 inches are for the bigger cars with minimal roof curvature and custom or commercial vans.

Figure 1-1 shows a typical 15″ × 30″ one-piece sunroof very popular with the Camaro and Firebird set. The one illustrated here was set in the roof of an older (pre-'82) Camaro. Note how well it fits and conforms to the roof curvature, a factor essential for minimizing leaks and metal kinks. Figure 1-2 shows the standard latching configuration that is also the one used in the sunroof in Fig. 1-1. A greater percentage of the one-piece sunroof manufacturers use this double (or single) latching technique. The latch both locks down the glass sunroof panel or holds it up at its maximum aperture as shown in Fig. 1-3.

MOON ROOFS

The so-called "moon roof" concept came into being in the 1970s when some enterprising designer came upon the idea (which probably came from T-tops) of mounting small sunroofs side by side. This tandem configuration used two 17″ × 17″ units mounted in pairs on larger cars and, more desirably, on pickups and vans. Some dual sunroofs (one common frame, two lifting panels) are called moon roofs, but this is not true in the exact sense of the term. Some manufacturers designate even the squarer looking one-piece

3

sunroofs as moon roofs, but in essence the true moon roofs are the small, square units mounted in a side-by-side mode. A number of manufacturers produce these minisunroofs and call them "moon roofs."

DUAL SUNROOFS

The dual, or "his-and-her" sunroof, is the newest of the pop-in sunroof designs featuring two operable glass panels sharing a common frame, Fig. 1-4. Either the driver or passenger panel, or both, can be opened to offer a dual ventilation option—moderate or maximum. An attractive crossbar incorporated into these units also helps enhance interior decor. The his-and-her sunroof is a very attractive design, and it is enjoying a surge in popularity.

ELECTRIC SUNROOFS

The electric sunroof is the epitome of sunroof excellence. It is highly sophisticated; the touch of a button opens it in controlled increments. This governs the amount of ventilation entering the car. Figure 1-5 shows a top-of-the-line Hollandia sunroof. Notice how the unit almost fits flush with the adjacent roof area, a desired feature of most custom-installed electric units.

The more luxurious electrics are slider types. These panels open and close with a back-and-forth (fully open to fully closed) sliding

Fig. 1-3. One-piece pop-up fully open.

4

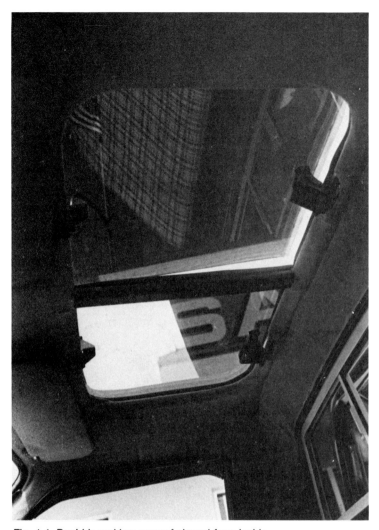

Fig. 1-4. Dual his-and-her sunroof viewed from inside.

action that is totally controlled by a motor. The sliding panel always remains level or parallel with the roof surface.

Two popular motor drives are used in modern electric sunroofs: a worm gear drive or a cable drive. In-depth analysis of electric sunroofs can be found in Chapter 7. Motor units are either integrally mounted in the sunroof assembly unit (at the rear) or remotely mounted using cables to control panel operation. The driver can control the sliding panel at the touch of a button (Fig. 1-6).

Fig. 1-5. Hollandia sliding electric sunroof. Courtesy Hollandia.

Fig. 1-6. Pushbutton in headliner panel controls opening action. Courtesy Hollandia.

6

Another type of electric sunroof is shown in Fig. 1-7. This unit, the Hollandia Sun-Slider, opens upward and back, out of the roof so to speak. Not as sophisticated as the slide type, it is nonetheless a highly efficient electric sunroof, reasonably priced, and attractive. It is gaining much acceptance in the compact and import car field.

T-TOPS

The T-tops are in a class by themselves because they all conform to the standard T-top configuration. T-tops are two pieces mounted separately on a common strengthening roof frame which, when in place, become a structural part of the car (roof). Because T-tops must be structurally sound and meet certain safety requirements, all the units produced to data are of fine quality, differing only in minor styling features. In true T-top installation, major surgery is performed on the roof, and a T-top retaining plate, or "backbone," must be fitted exactly.

The T-top is so-called because the roof (when the glass panels are removed) takes on a T-shape when viewed from the top of the vehicle (Fig. 1-8). A number of people also feel that the T stands for twin. Both hypothetical statements can and do apply.

In most cases, T-tops are not as readily available to the public as pop-in sunroofs because they must be properly, professionally, and exactingly installed to avoid irreparable damage to the vehi-

Fig. 1-7. The Sun Slider model in open mode. Courtesy Hollandia.

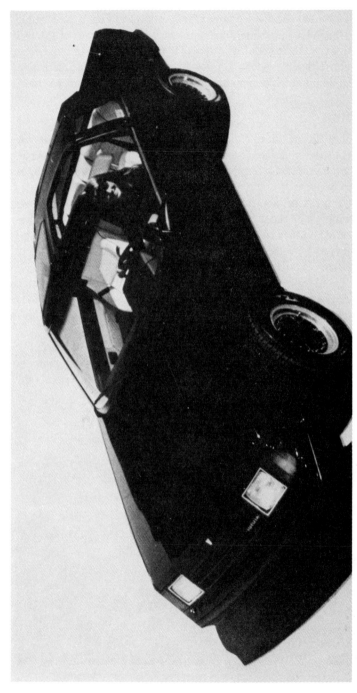

Fig. 1-8. Pacific T-top unit mounted in 1983 Toyota Celica.

cle's roof. T-tops and installation services are available nationally at franchised dealers. See Chapters 2 and 6 for particulars on T-tops and their installation requirements.

Chapter 2

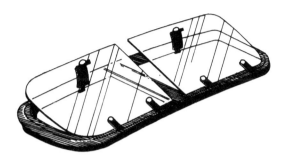

Manufacturers and Suppliers

Fortunately for all prospective buyers, 99.9 percent of manufacturers producing T-tops and sunroofs have created quality products. Some might be easier to install or look better than others, and some may suit individual requirements better than others. All will serve the consumer well, however.

The manufacturers and suppliers listed in this chapter all produce and/or distribute high-quality items. All are highly recommended. Final selection if governed by personal preferences and size or shape requirements.

All products listed can be purchased at local specialty auto suppliers or van shops, often on a special order basis. If you cannot obtain satisfaction locally, you can contact and, in most instances, order directly from the sources listed here.

SUNROOFS

The following manufacturers and suppliers make and/or distribute manual sunroofs.

Stretch Forming Corporation
10870 Talbert Ave.
Fountain Valley, CA 92708

Stretch Forming has been an innovative leader in the field of sunroofs and specialty windows for over a decade. Six styles of sunroofs in various sizes are offered by this company.

Available for the larger vans, the *Autoport Van Sunroofs* come in 15″ × 30″ and 17″ × 35″ sizes. A special feature of the Stretch Forming Autoports (if desired as an option) is preformed grooves to accommodate the protruding roof ribs on many van types. This gives a more positive, leakproof fit. Figure 2-1 shows the Autoport Van Sunroof styling. Autoport glass features a special permanently bonded tint screen that lets through the sunlight, but not the heat.

The *Autoport I* (Fig. 2-2) is a compact, single-latch model available in 15″ × 30″ and 17″ × 35″ sizes with optional black or polished trim. The reflective glass panels can be removed from the inside for increased ventilation.

The *Dual Autoport II* (Fig. 2-3) is a tandem glass sunroof sharing a common frame. Each side can be opened individually when you prefer. This unit is available in 17″ × 35″ or 20″ × 37″ sizes. Frame options are black or polished trim. The *"his-and-hers"* dual version consist of two separate pieces that are mounted side by side. Each unit of the pair measures 17″ × 17″.

A small unit or minisunroof (Fig. 2-4) is also marketed primarily for use in vans as an auxiliary venting unit. The *Vent Sunroof* is 17″ × 17″.

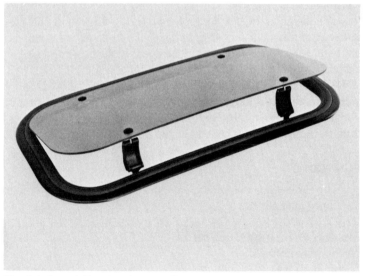

Fig. 2-1. Stretch Forming Autoport II.

Fig. 2-2. Stretch Forming Single-Latch Autoport.

Added features of the Stretch Forming units include silicone sealing and positive rear main latches that stay in the glass sections when they are removed. The front hinge latches have easy-to-operate locking levers that release from the glass by means of release tabs. Stretch Forming also makes a specially designed sunroof for the Volkswagon Beetle.

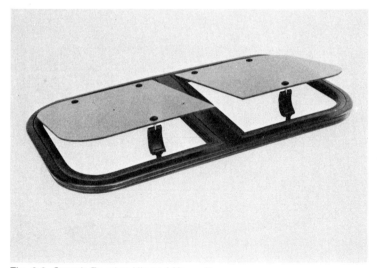

Fig. 2-3. Stretch Forming His-and Her unit.

Fig. 2-4. Stretch Forming Mini-Sunroof.

Interpart Corporation
230 W. Rosecrans Ave.
Gardena, CA 90248

Interpart is one of the newer companies getting involved in sunroof manufacture and distribution. Its Lifttop line offers two basic

Fig. 2-5. Interpret One-Piece Lifttop.

14

types of sunroofs: the universal model for most cars, minitrucks and vans for mounting in thin wall roofs and a universal model for vans or vehicles with headliners thicker than 5/8 of an inch. Interpart also markets a special one-piece sunroof for the VW Beetle and Super Beetle, all years.

The two sunroof styles in the Interpart line include the standard one-piece *Lifttop* (Fig. 2-5) and the *Twin-Top Lifttop* version. The one-piece Lifttop is available in three sizes: 15″ × 30″, 17″ × 30″, and 20″ × 34″. The Twin-Top model is 20″ × 34″ (Fig. 2-6). The unusually sized VW Beetle sunroof is 16″ × 25″.

The Interpart sunroof glass in all models is reflective, solar-resistant, that is, it has a permanently bonded reflective finish to curtail the heat of the sun. This reflective glass, 3/16″ thick in all models, is said to block out 93 percent of the sun's heat. Frames are roof contoured and mounted flush. Glass panels in both single and dual units are fully removable and replaceable.

Production Research
107 W. Alexis Rd.
Toledo, OH 43612

Production Research sunroofs come in two sizes, 16″ × 30″ and 17″ × 35″ in single-latch or double-latch versions (Fig. 2-7). All models feature safety-tempered, solar-cool, bronze-tinted glass

Fig. 2-6. Interpret Twin Lifttop.

Fig. 2-7. Production Research 16″ × 30″.

and long-life rubber gaskets. Glass is removable. The smaller model is very popular with older-style Camaro and Firebird owners.

Hammond Manufacturing Corporation
Box 11007
Lansing, MI 48901

Hammond has long been a leader in the sunroof and van-window field. It is probably one of the oldest suppliers specializing in products for the recreational vehicle and custom-van field. Its sunroofs are very sturdy and durable and are offered in five sizes, making them universally applicable in virtually all situations.

The larger Hammond sunroof ideal for van installation (Fig. 2-8) features a removable all-acrylic cover available in three colors: smoke, gold, and blue. The cover features snap-in installation, dual arms, and single actuator opening. A screen unit is available as an accessory.

Other popular models include the 17″ × 35″ single-glass-panel unit featuring universal-van-style trim rings and frame-finish options of black or chrome. The 17″ × 35″ *Twin Port* (glass) model for individual driver or passenger usage (Fig. 2-9) has an optional black or bright frame. The one-piece glass units for compact and midsize cars come with optional black or silver universal trim rings and in 15″ × 30″ and 16″ × 30″ sizes.

The newest addition to the Hammond line is the *Classic Hammond Miniroof* model (Fig. 2-10). The Miniroof features a 15″×-16″

Fig. 2-8. Hammond RV Sunroof.

custom-contoured acrylic plastic dome in three color options: smoke, gold, or blue. It is ideally suited for single his-and-her application or as an auxiliary back vent used for upgrading ventilation in conjunction with a forward-mounted sunroof. In addition, Hammond markets auxiliary venting accessories, such as the *Vanvent* (Fig. 2-11), and a variety of exhaust units. When used with the sunroofs, these accessories help upgrade ventilation facilities of vans and larger type vehicles.

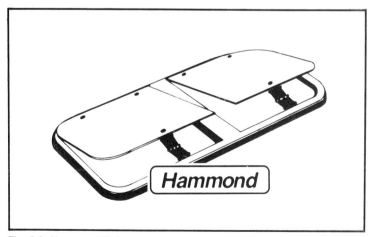

Fig. 2-9. Hammond Twin.

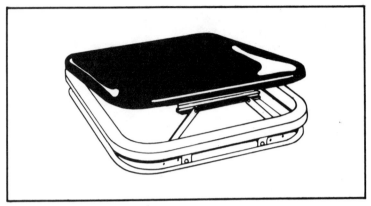

Fig. 2-10. Classic Hammond Miniroof.

Elixir Industries
17809 S. Broadway
Gardena, CA 90248

Elixir is another accredited manufacturer and distributor of fine-quality sunroofs and windows. Three of their excellent sunroof models are illustrated in Fig. 2-12. The *Astra-View Double Latch* model features two latch locking facilities for positive fit and comes in two sizes: 15″ × 30″ and 17″ × 35″. The *Astra-View Single Latch* models also come in the same size options as the double-latch units. A split-top sunroof model, the *Astra II View*, comes in a 17″ × 35″

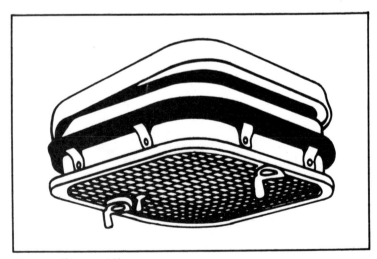

Fig. 2-11. Hammond Vanvent.

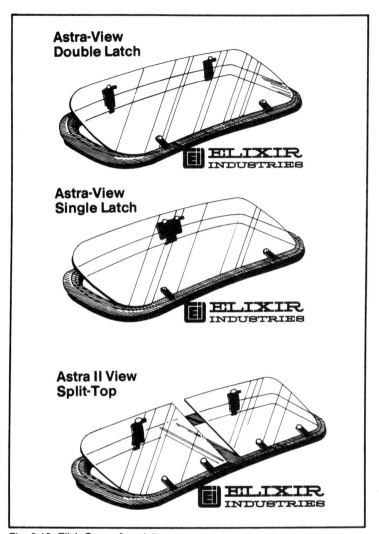

**Astra-View
Double Latch**

EI ELIXIR
INDUSTRIES

**Astra-View
Single Latch**

EI ELIXIR
INDUSTRIES

**Astra II View
Split-Top**

EI ELIXIR
INDUSTRIES

Fig. 2-12. Elixir Sunroof models.

size and features an internal accessory item—a wide light bar with a 12-volt light source that can be attached to existing electrical wiring. The *Astra View Compact* 17" × 17" units can be mounted singly or in pairs (his-and-hers model). The *Elixir Day *Star* sunroof, designed expressly for the VW Beetle, has a low profile and is contoured for most Beetle models. All Elixir sunroof models feature removable, reflective solar glass tops and optional choice of black or polished frames.

Guaranteed Products
355 N. Vineland Ave.
City of Industry, CA 91749

Not extensively into the sunroof business, Guaranteed Products does offer two model sizes in sunroofs: a 15" × 30" unit and a 17" × 35" unit. Both sizes are designed for use on 90 percent of the cars on the road. Guaranteed Products sunroofs contain reflective glass panels, an adjustable single-action handle, a universal trim ring for installation ease, and a vinyl screw cover to enhance appearance.

Excel Industries of California
12661 Box Springs Blvd.
Riverside, CA 92507

Originally an OEM source, Excel has now made its sunroofs available to the aftermarket purchasing public. Excel sunroofs come in four sizes for universal appeal: 17" × 15", 17" × 27", 17" × 31", 17" × 35". All models feature a clamp like system, heavy-duty aluminum frames, and removable solar-reflecting safety glass.

Prestige Aluminum Products
10639 Ramona Ave.
Montclair, CA 91763

This quality producer presents an excellent product with a few novel aspects. The *Prestige #1100* sunroof was designed for universal application (Fig. 2-13). Its 16" × 32" size fits in many domestic and foreign cars and trucks. It has an original-equipment styling appearance, low-profile, factory look. It is one of the few aftermarket accessory sunroofs with deep compound curved glass. The Prestige sunroof contains a high-pressure, injection-molded frame with a low-profile, sculptured wind deflector on the leading edge to minimize wind resistance and noise. The Prestige Sunroof comes in a black frame finish and also features spring-loaded slide latches.

West Coast Sunroofs
1007-B Melrose Street
Placentia, CA 92670

West Coast produces an ideal little sunroof. Two universal sizes

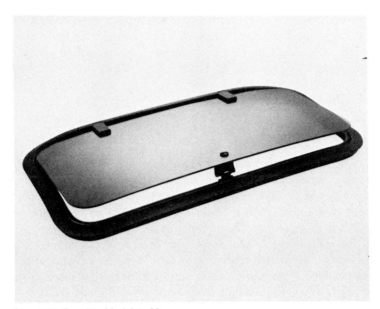

Fig. 2-13. Prestige Model 1100.

are marketed by the company: a 15″ × 30″ single-latch and a 17″ × 35″ double-latch type (Fig. 2-14). The highly efficient, solar-resisting glass panels inhibit 90 percent of the sun's heat and are removable. These sunroofs are assembled with chrome-plated brass

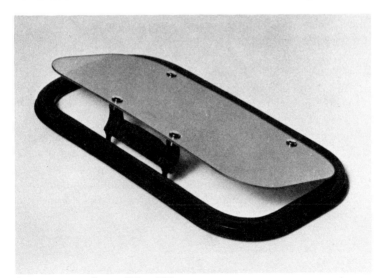

Fig. 2-14. West Coast 15″ × 30″.

hardware that is impervious to rust and retains overall brilliance. As an option, an accessory sunshield is also offered if total blockage of light is desired. The West Coast Sunset Sunroofs will fit virtually all vehicles.

Le Van Specialty Company
P.O. Box 2159
City of Industry, CA 92746

Le Van is another manufacture of sunroofs and specialty windows, primarily for the van aficionados. Le Van offers a wide array of single and his-and-her sunroofs, moonroofs, and miniroofs in a wide assortment of sizes. Models feature tinted and clear solar-resistant glass, removable and replaceable. A favorite among VW Beetle buffs is the *Le Van Beetle* sunroof, specially contoured for the excessively curved roof of the older VW models. A special inner headliner trim ring accommodates a narrow vinyl insert that completely covers retaining screws and gives a clean OEM appearance.

Pacific
15241 Transistor Lane
Huntington Beach, CA 92649

Pacific boasts that it is the "World's Largest T-top/Moonroof Center." It deals in optimum quality products and has a vast line of aftermarket custom additive accessories.

Pacific markets an exceptionally fine, magnificently styled sunroof called the *RX-7 Moonroof* (Fig. 2-15). The RX-7 is completely assembled and installs quickly and easily without major surgery to the roof involved. The *Pacific Moonroof* is an easy swap RX-7 replacement part which can replace the present factory-removable steel panel version. The Moonroof features reflective-coated, solar-cool grey, tempered safety glass with a special ceramic sun screen coated onto the glass and around the perimeter to conceal the roof drain channels. The RX-7 Moonroof offers substantially upgraded visibility without leakage, wind noise, or unsightly trim ring around the edge.

C.R. Laurence Co., Inc.
2503 E. Vernon Ave.
Los Angeles, CA 90058-1897

Fig. 2-15. Pacific RX-7 Sunroof.

C.R. Laurence company is well known and respected in glazing, industrial construction, and automotive supplies. It is now channeling its expertise into the sunroof market, producing high-quality aftermarket one-piece, dual, and tandem mount units. The following units are in the *Sunstyle* line.

The one-piece, single-glass *Sunstyle Sunroof* is available in two sizes: 15″ × 30″ and 17″ × 35″. This model comes in a black or polished frame with new ceramic matrix coatings to guard against scratching (Fig. 2-16). A new six-position handle, is a recent option for this model.

The *Sunstyle T-Port* is the dual his-and-her version in the 17″ × 35″ size only (Fig. 2-17). These units also offer a new lighted center bar in the interior frame piece (Fig. 2-18). Frame finish choices are polished or black.

The *Sunstyle Double-Glass Sunroofs,* one of the few tandem-mount sunroofs available (Fig. 2-19), are unusual and highly preferred by custom van and pickup owners. Each of the units measures 17″ × 17″ and come with black frames.

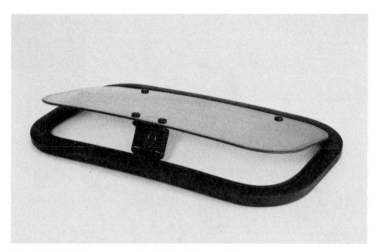

Fig. 2-16. C.R. Laurence single Sunstyle model.

Cars & Concepts Inc.
12500 E. Grand River
Brighton, MI 48116

An active and recognized producer of quality T-tops, Cars & Concepts also markets an excellent one-piece sunroof (Fig. 2-20) universally applicable to all cars, vans, and pickups. The handsome, well-designed, and conceived sunroof is removable. The frame is vented and provides positive drainage outlets which release and drain water through car door frame posts. Frames are black.

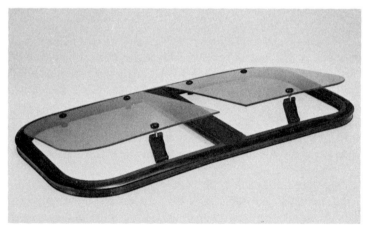

Fig. 2-17. C.R. Laurence Sunstyle T-Port.

24

Fig. 2-18. C.R. Laurence Sunstyle T-Port interior side showing bar light.

ELECTRIC SUNROOFS

Though there are not as many electric sunroof manufacturers as manual sunroof manufacturers, the few companies involved offer highly sophisticated models. These electrified versions are the epitome of sunroof excellence.

American Sunroof
1862 S. La Cienega
Los Angeles, CA 90035

American is the prominent domestic manufacturer of electric sunroofs, providing universal aftermarket installation through a national dealer network. The *Sungazer* is a steel sunroof that flush

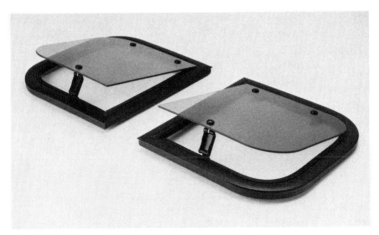

Fig. 2-19. C.R. Laurence Sunstyle Double-Glass Sunroof.

Fig. 2-20. Cars & Concepts Sunroof.

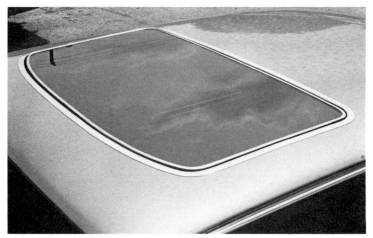

Fig. 2-21. American Stargazer Sunroof.

fits in the roof of all foreign and domestic cars and gives an OEM finished look. The panel opens at the flip of a switch. The frame contains an anodized peripheral molding or trim edging that enhances roof appearance.

The *Stargazer* model is similar in quality and function to the Sungazer. It includes a reflective glass panel as opposed to the steel panel. The glass sunroof panel is available in silver or gold; the colors aid in reflecting the sun's heat (Fig. 2-21). An intergrated sunshade slider allows closing off of the entire roof opening. Figure 2-22 shows the Stargazer in full open position.

Fig. 2-22. American Stargazer, open position.

27

Fig. 2-23. Hollandia Sun Slider.

Hollandia-Sunroofs Inc.
10080 Sumac Circle
Eden Prairie, MN 55344

The oldest, most prominent, and finest manufacturer of optimum quality electric sunroofs is Hollandia, an American distributorship with its home base and manufacturing facilities in the Netherlands. Hollandia offers a few electric models in two stylings that have gained them worldwide acceptance and popularity.

The *Sun-Slider* (Fig. 2-23) features flush fit mounting on virtually all cars, including many domestic and imported compacts. It is one of the best-looking, and best-operating sunroofs to date, and it is reasonably priced to boot. The 17 1/2″ × 32″ unit contains heat-resistant glass and integrated drain tubes. The Sun-Slider opens to a width of 8 1/2″ (Fig. 2-24), and a special overhead turning knob allows the glass panel section to tilt as well as slide for varying degrees of ventilation. Figure 2-25 shows the interior control panel that also helps enhance interior decor. An optional wind deflector unit is also offered by the company (Fig. 2-26). For the budget minded, a similar manually operated version of the Sun-Slider is available.

Top-of-the-line Hollandia sunroofs are the electric glasstop versions, the finest units of this type manufactured to date (Fig. 2-27). These sunroofs offer thin housings, specially patented wind deflectors, interchangeable steel or glass panels, one-piece polished

Fig. 2-24. Sun Slider open.

stainless steel frames, two types of drive systems (see Chapter 7, Electric Sunroofs), quiet motor operation, integrated sunshades, and an internal drainage system. Glasstop models contain one-way, mirror-type, shatterproof glass. Hollandia's glasstop model sliding roofs are available in the following sizes fitting almost all types of

Fig. 2-25. Hollandia control panel.

Fig. 2-26. Hollandia Sun Slider wind deflector.

foreign and domestic vehicles: Model 71—17″ × 32 1/2″, Model 72—17″ × 35 1/2″, Model 77—17″ × 39″, and 79—21″ × 39″. Figure 2-28 shows the Hollandia Sliding glass sunroof in its open position.

T-TOPS

T-tops are in a class by themselves. They are primarily designed for ventilation, they have a unique and sporty appearance

Fig. 2-27. Hollandia Electric Sliding Sunroof.

Fig. 2-28. Hollandia Electric Sliding Sunroof, open position.

and do much to enhance and customize the outer appearance of the car. Since the T-top and its installation is so complex, it is strongly recommended that T-top installation be undertaken only by qualified experts. Here are the leading T-top manufacturers and installation services available to the public through a nationwide dealer franchise services.

Cars & Concepts Inc.
12500 E. Grand River Ave.
Brighton, MI 48116

Specially designed by Cars & Concepts, the *Skylite T-Roof* achieves a novel integrated look complimenting the design and appearance of the car in which it is installed. Cars & Concepts T-top glass panels feature solar-reflective tempered glass controlling sunlight and interior heat buildup. The T-top panels release easily with a single hand-latch mechanism. Also included are two padded vinyl pouches for storage and protection when the T-tops are removed. Cars & Concepts T-tops are available for the following cars:

Chevrolet Camaro	(73-83)
Pontiac Firebird	(73-83)
Chev. Monte Carlo	(78-83)
Oldsmobile Cutlass	(78-83)

Fig. 2-29. Cars & Concepts Skylight T-Roof on a 1983 Camaro.

Fig. 2-30. Pacific T-top in 1983 Datsun 200 SX.

33

Buick Regal	(78-83)
Pontiac Grand Prix	(78-83)
Ford Mustang	(79-83)
Mercury Capri	(79-83)
Dodge Aspen	(77-83)
Plymouth Volare	(77-83)
Dodge Mirada	(80-83)
Chrysler Cordoba	(80-83)

Figure 2-29 illustrates the stylish Cars & Concepts T-top installed in the 1983 Camaro.

Pacific
15241 Transistor Lane
Huntington Beach, CA 92649

Pacific is another prominent T-top manufacturer concentrating mainly on the Japanese import car field. Pacific T-tops provide a national dealer network specializing in T-top insertion in Toyota Celicas, Supras, Datsun, etc. Figure 2-30 shows a typical Japanese import treatment with the T-top package. Pacific stocks a full line of T-top replacement parts for factory installed T-tops for other non-factory brands.

Chapter 3

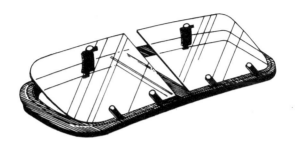

Sunroof Mounting Basics

The home brew approach to installation of the more radical of
sophisticated sunroofs (internal draining, electric, T-top) is not
recommended for the average do-it-yourselfer and should only be
undertaken by professional people. The simpler one-piece, pop-in
sunroofs can easily be installed by the average person, however.
Before undertaking even this simpler approach, the neophyte should
familiarize himself with preliminary considerations and requirements.

SELECTING A SUNROOF

When selecting a sunroof for your particular vehicle, the first
thing to consider is the appropriate size. Too many people opt for
the largest possible size, which may fit into the roof area but creates
havoc when tightened down. Roof pitch and roof curvature must
be studied. If the sunroof is too large, or if the curvature of the
sunroof frame does not properly conform to the roof contours,
disastrous buckling of the outlying metal areas will occur.

Prior to selecting a sunroof, check manufacturers' literature and
study Chapter 2 thoroughly. If possible, choose a model that is
recommended for a specific car or vehicle type. The manufacturer
will usually state its product's application requirements in its
literature.

CENTERING THE SUNROOF

Figure 3-1 is a typical roof planning diagram that shows how to properly place the sunroof to be installed. To arrive at the proper centering locations, first establish the center line of the vehicle (V.C.L.) by measuring across the roof from drip rail to drip rail and dividing by two. The template usually provided with the sunroof should then be aligned exactly to the established vehicle center line marks placed on the roof. The distance (D) from the top border molding of the windshield is then determined by selecting the "D"

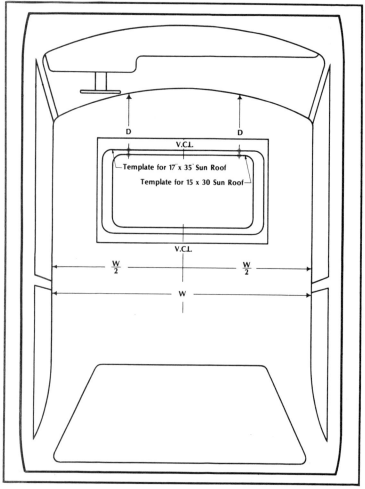

Fig. 3-1. How to determine best sunroof location. Courtesy Stretch Forming Corporation.

dimensions recommended by the manufacturer in its installation diagrams or measurement charts.

Dimensions established should also take into account location of headliner and seams, interior roof lights, and headliner braces or bows if any exist. With most vehicles there is a bit of latitude in these dimensions, whether minimal or maximal. The major leeway is in the forward or backward placement of the sunroof according to individual taste. Also consider a vinyl half-roof, if one exists on the car. When placing a sunroof in a half-top situation, take the extent of the covered area into account.

ROOF THICKNESS

The roof thickness is another critical factor that must be evaluated. Vehicles today, whether cars, vans, or trucks, usually have three common structural roof thickness configurations. They are:

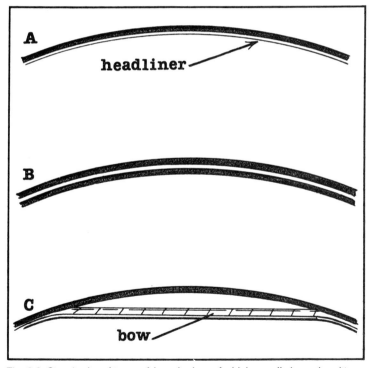

Fig. 3-2. Standard roof types. *A* is a single roof which usually has a headliner bonded to the inner side. *B* is the double steel roof. The headliner is attached to the bottom of the second inner metal sheet. In *C* bows or struts space the headliner from the roof metal to obtain headliner depth.

1. Single steel with a bonded headliner.
2. Double steel with bonded or fastened headliner.
3. Single steel with bow headliner spacer. Bows are usually steel rods or straps.

Figure 3-2 shows cross sections of these typical roof-headliner composites. A shows a single steel roof with a bonded headliner underneath. B is a double steel roof in which the inner roof sheeting runs parallel to the upper. The headliner is usually bonded to the bottom steel sheathing in the same manner as in A.

In some instances (such as in some rare single steel roofs), there may be some welded-on bracing or channelling for rigidity. These may have to be ground or shaved down around the roof opening if they interfere with the sunroof trim or garnish ring.

Remember to take into account roof thickness when preparing for installation. This added consideration is second in importance to sunroof-to-roof centering preliminaries.

FRAMES AND GARNISH RINGS

The type and width of the sunroof frame or ring is also a primary factor in selecting a sunroof. Most manufacturers include built-in variables for universal mounting applications. Some manufacturers offer frames in varied standard widths, some with universally adaptable frames and a few mass producers have both.

Figure 3-3 illustrates this best. The three top trim-rings are standard width types that are produced by the sunroof industry (with minor variations between manufacturers) and their application in typical roof thickness circumstances. The three lower illustrations feature the Stretch Forming universal trim-ring concept pioneered by the company. They afford the consumer the best and most positive alternatives in universal sunroof mounting.

The universal Stretch Forming trim-ring is ready to mount and can accommodate both thin or single steel roofs with no modifications. To accommodate widths varying from 3/8″ to 5/8″, the Stretch Forming 05 and 06 trim-rings are more flexible. Their ring spacing can be adapted to conform to the thicker roof-headliner widths with minor modification. The ring contains two grooves running around the entire perimeter. If extra thickness or spacing is required between frame and roof steel, modify the ring piece for a 3/8″ or 5/8″ desired width by piercing or cutting at the required space groove with a pair of dykes or snips. Use a pair of pliers to twist

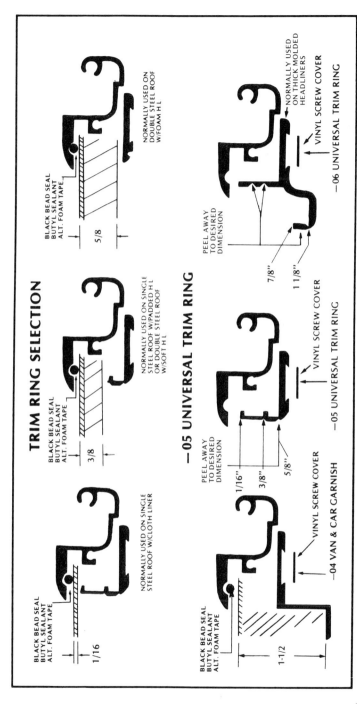

Fig. 3-3. Typical garnish ring configurations. Courtesy Stretch Forming Corporation.

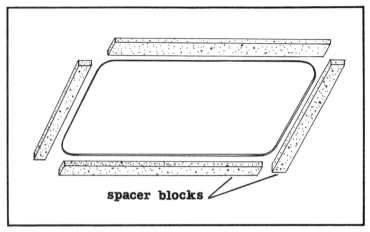

Fig. 3-4. The use of spacer blocks to obtain spacing and proper fit between sunroof trim ring and roof.

away and remove additional strip thickness. Then file the remaining rough edge smooth. Both 05 to 06 Stretch Forming trim-rings can be modified in this fashion. This is a most rewarding facet to incorporate as a sunroof adaptability feature.

If other than a preassembled trim-ring is used to mount your sunroof, be sure to size and space it by preassembly prior to installing the sunroof into the roof. The ring should be positioned and sized before cutting the trim-ring. This will guarantee proper fit and sealing.

In some instances, inserting spacer blocks between headliner and roof may be required to build up proper spacing as well as a firm fit between trim-ring and inner roof (headliner) surface. Insert spacer blocks under the roof around the cut opening as shown in Fig. 3-4. These space block (of the proper width) may be cut from wood or Homosote. The best medium to use for spacing is Styrofoam available in widths from 1/4″ on up. Styrofoam has enough rigidity, yet will give a little when the trim-ring is tightened down, assuring a positive, secure fit.

INSTALLATION TIPS

A step-by-step mounting procedure and visual presentation of a typical sunroof installation is presented in Chapter 4. Here are a few addition tips to aid the do-it-yourselfer:

☐ Check to see if a dome light is located within the perimeter

40

where the sunroof will be mounted. If one exists, it will have to be removed and discarded or relocated.

☐ If your vehicle has a roof luggage rack, make sure it does not interfere with the proposed sunroof location. See that internal roof braces (if any exist) do not interfere with sunroof mounting.

☐ When trimming Styrofoam for spacing or headliners, a heated knife will help you obtain smooth, clean cuts.

☐ Cloth headliners affixed to their foam backings may be separated from the foam by applying alcohol. The alcohol is best applied by spray with an atomizer. After the cloth is loosened, it may be peeled back and the foam trimmed as desired. As the alcohol dries, the bonding in adjacent unpeeled areas will remain secure.

☐ If you wish to check headliner thickness or spacing before cutting into it or the roof, use a needle to penetrate into the headliner. Marking the depth of penetration on the needle will give you the exact depth measurement.

WATER DRAINAGE

All sunroofs today have water control and drainage facilities so that water will not fall into the car when the sunroof is opened after a rainfall. Some have simple drainage outlets and some have more effective run-off facilities.

A more sophisticated system not found on many pop-in sunroof systems is the one shown in Fig. 3-5. This sunroof unit, one of the finest, is marketed by Cars & Concepts. It contains a special draining trough. Water buildup is dispelled through corner-mounted drain tubes which are concealed between the roof and headliner after the sunroof is mounted in place. These tubes allow water to drain through the front and middle door frame to under the car. These channels (or pillars) are a unique drainage concept.

SEALING THE SUNROOF

Certain sealing procedures and precautions must be exercised as part of sunroof installation. The area of contact between the sunroof frame and upper roof surface must be hermetically sealed to weatherproof the driver's compartment. No matter how tight or snug the sunroof fits, some form of sealing must take place. The following methods are acknowledged as the best methods.

Recreational Vehicle Window Sealer. Nicknames in van circles "Gorilla Snot," this is a grey, puttylike sealant that remains

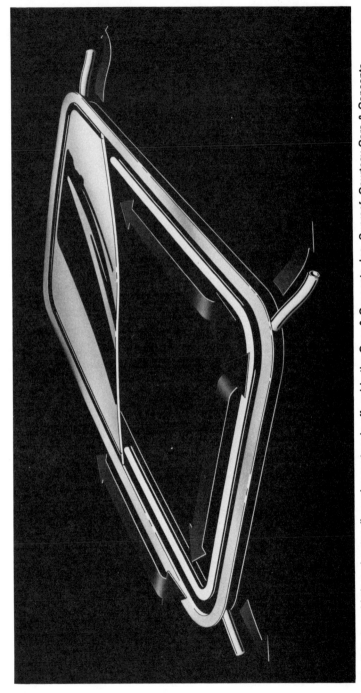

Fig. 3-5. A sophisticated water dispersion system is offered in the Cars & Concepts, Inc. Sunroof. Courtesy Cars & Concepts.

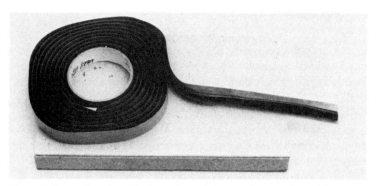

Fig. 3-6. Sunroof sealer strip is packaged with most sunroofs and is an excellent sealing medium.

soft and has maximum give when securing down a window frame. Originally marketed for mounting large van windows, it can also be used as a sealant for sunroofs. Its negative factors are it's messy, uncontrollable, and has a tendency to continue to ooze out for long periods after the window is mounted. It always retains its soft, oozy state which is heightened by sun and heat.

Black Sealer Strip. This Butyl-type material (Fig. 3-6) comes with all sunroof kits. It is the most workable, best sealing medium to date. It has the right "give" property and affords excellent adhesion and weatherproofing.

Fig. 3-7. Windo-Weld Sealer (left) and Duro Weatherstrip Cement (right) are both useful for sealing. Windo-Weld is very thick and firmer than most Butyl sealants.

Windo-Weld Stripping. Primarily designed as an auto windshield sealer, it is very thick and strong, also Butyl. Not as desirable or as efficient as sealer-strip, it is most applicable in sunroof sealing situations in which there is some frame-to-roof fit discrepancy. Windo-Weld is much thicker and less pliable than the thinner roof sealing medium; its a bulkier type strip material. It must be used with Windo-Weld sealer, a liquid gluelike substance that is applied with a brush over surfaces on which Windo-Weld stripping will be applied. Windo-Weld Stripping and a standard weather stripping cement are shown in Fig. 3-7.

Prior to applying any of the sealer strips mentioned it is advisable to brush coat the metal and frame contact surfaces with weatherstrip cement. This will further guard against possible water leakage.

Chapter 4

Sunroof Installation

The basic, all-in-one, pop-in sunroof is usually a standardized unit that is fairly simple to install. Most of these sunroofs measure approximately 15" × 30" to 17" × 35". They fit or adapt to virtually all cars, trucks, and vans, except for such cars as the Volkswagen Beetle, which has a radically curved roof. For this reason, a specific sunroof is marketed exclusively for the Volkswagen "bug".

This chapter describes a typical sunroof installation featuring the 15" × 30" Stretch Forming Sunroof, one of the finest and easiest to install on the market. This model, a small compact unit, was installed on a Chevy Luv pickup truck. Though the exact mounting methods may vary from vehicle to vehicle and the particular sunroof involved, this procedure will provide an in-depth study of what installing drop-in sunroofs is all about.

TOOLING

All integrated mounting structural pieces for sunroof installation are provided by sunroof manufacturers. Once the proper sunroof has been purchased, the only additional equipment needed are the cutting tools to cut an opening in the roof to secure and mount the sunroof.

The first tool needed is a basic *electric drill*. A typical drill found in most households will do. The drill is used to drill out the preliminary access hole for a cutting utensil, which will then be used to cut the opening. Other simple items to have on hand include narrow masking tape, a line striker (or if you prefer, marking crayons), and a ruler or tape measure.

For cutting the basic opening, the following tools are recommended:

Air scissors or shears (Fig. 4-1) is a good tool if you have access to it and an air compressor. The air-driven scissor tips cut through metal quickly, allowing accurate and even cutting.

The *nibbler* is another air-powered (or electric) tool. It acts differently than most cutters in that it achieves its cutting action by chipping away the metal in small, progressive increments until a cut is made. Some expertise is necessary for handling the nibbler. It makes a wide cut, and one must cut on the inner side of the designated opening marks or the opening will be off-size.

The jigsaw is the most recommended tool for the neophyte. The jigsaw is a standard homeowner tool. It works very well for cutting steel and doesn't have a tendency to run away from you if it is carefully manipulated and guided. Even the most simple and basic jigsaw (Fig. 4-2) will do the job efficiently. When choosing saw blades, pick the best high-tempered steel types. For standard automotive-type sheet metal, a blade with 24 to 32 teeth per inch is recommended. For thicker metals, a blade with 18 teeth to the inch is advised. One good, new blade should do the job nicely. Keep an extra one on hand

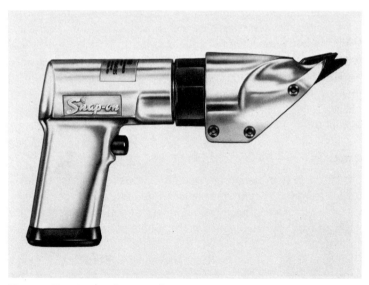

Fig. 4-1. Air scissors. Courtesy Snap-On-Tools.

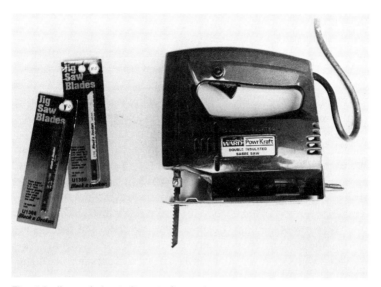

Fig. 4-2. Jigsaw is best alternate for cutting.

if your main blade breaks. (This can happen easily when cutting steel.) Blades with less than 18 teeth per inch are not recommended. They are solely for cutting wood or composite materials.

In our described installation, we utilized a small jigsaw and 32-tooth blades. The blades were high-temper steel by Black & Decker, which seem to be the best cutting and most durable.

POSITIONING THE SUNROOF

The first step is to clean the roof with soap and water or wax and grease remover to allow good marker or tape adhesion when laying out the opening marker lines. If the inside of the car (roof or headliner) contains an interior light, it should be disconnected and removed. (It can be relocated later if desired.)

Check and study the headliner. Cut away a small section toward the middle of the sunroof location so you can study the roof-headliner structure. A cloth or vinyl headliner opening must be cut separately from the roof opening. A hard headliner, or one attached directly to the roof metal, will allow the roof and headliner opening to be cut at the same time using a standard length cutting blade. In the Chevy Luv truck, the inner headliner and the roof are separate, with spacing provided by bows or rods that span across the inside of the roof. Any of the bows falling within the perimeter of the sunroof opening were removed and discarded.

With this sunroof (as with most manufacturers), an explicit set of mounting instructions, hardware, sealant, and templates is included (Fig. 4-3). The instructions should be studied carefully to compensate for possible variations between automobile and sunroof models (size, type, etc.).

The first step in cutting the roof opening is the most crucial—positioning. The opening must be perfectly centered for proper sunroof alignment.

Measurements must be taken on all sides and a center line struck that aligns with the opening template center line provided on the manufacturer's template (Figs. 4-4, 4-5, 4-6). After you have done the measuring procedure once, do it again to double check. We cannot stress how important it is to properly measure and position the required opening. It can only be cut once, and there is little remedy for a botched-up job.

Once a center line and accurate measurements are obtained, secure the template provided by the manufacturer to the roof with tape. The template provided by Stretch Forming is on the installation instruction sheet and can be cut out and placed on the roof for the initial layout. Once the template is positioned, trace the outline *accurately* with 1/4-inch masking tape as shown in Fig. 4-7. Figure 4-8 illustrates the tape outline.

CUTTING THE ROOF

Cutting procedures may now begin. The access hole for the

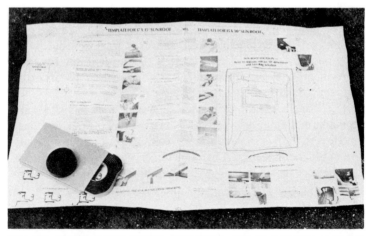

Fig. 4-3. Manufacturers provide instructions and all mounting materials necessary.

Fig. 4-4. Measuring the front roof line and center line evaluations.

Fig. 4-5. Measuring off the back border.

jigsaw must first be made. With a drill mounting a 3/8-inch bit, drill a hole into any one of the corners, just before the curve on the *inside* of the tape (Fig. 4-9). Place the blade of the saw into the drilled access hole and commence cutting out the opening slowly and carefully right against the inside edge of the tape (Fig. 4-10).

After the opening is cut out, remove the garnish or trim ring from the sunroof and place it in the roof opening to check for a proper fit. If the fit is a little bit loose (no more than 1/16 inch) on two sides, you are a bit off but still safe. If the fit is too snug, and the frame has to be forced, you are still safe; all you need do is expand the opening a trifle. This is best accomplished by grinding down the tight areas with a carborundum grinder, or "lollipop," placed in and powered by the same hand drill utilized to cut the preliminary access hole (Fig. 4-11).

Cutting the headliner is the next step in the installation procedure. Cut an initial access slit in the headliner (Fig. 4-12) using an X-Acto knife or razor blade. The truck shown here utilizes bows or rods to achieve roof-to-headliner spacing. One central bow is removed and the headliner opening cut to conform with the roof opening, but with a 1 1/2-inch border from the roof line edge alotted as in Fig. 4-13.

INSTALLING THE SUNROOF

The trim ring telescopes over the sunroof edge frame to secure

Fig. 4-6. Striking the center line.

Fig. 4-7. Securing the template and taping the outline.

it from the inner side. Remove it and prepare the main frame and glass (sunroof) section for insertion in the cab roof. Turn the sunroof frame (top down) on a cloth to avoid scratching the glass and apply a thin layer of weatherstrip cement around the frame (Fig. 4-14). This will aid in final weatherproof sealing adhesion of the black sealer material which must be affixed next all around the frame.

Fig. 4-8. Tape line layed out.

Fig. 4-9. Drilling the access hole for saw.

Fig. 4-10. Cutting the opening.

Take the sealer (paper-backed for protection) and apply it all around the inner side of the frame as shown in Fig. 4-15. The sealant, with the help of the weatherstrip adhesive already applied, should adhere firmly and positively to the frame.

The sunroof (with the sealer affixed) is then placed into the roof opening. Press down firmly around the peripheral areas of the sunroof frame. Do not press too hard or you will buckle or damage the roof which gives easily without the inner securing garnish ring attached (Fig. 4-16).

SECURING THE SUNROOF

At this point, installation is almost complete. Securing the sunroof is the final step of this simplified procedure.

Slip the trim ring around the frame edge protruding into the roof opening from the inside of the vehicle. Go around the ring securing it to the main sunroof frame with the Phillips-head screws provided (Fig. 4-17).

Trim rings provided with sunroof are adaptable to specific size and spacing requirements of varying roofs. Along the width of the trim ring are grooves allowing portions of the trim ring to be removed to regulate spacing. This is covered in depth in Chapter 3, Sunroof Basics.

As the screws on the trim ring are tightened fully, the two sides

Fig. 4-11. Trimming and sizing the edges.

55

Fig. 4-12. Cutting the access hole in headliner.

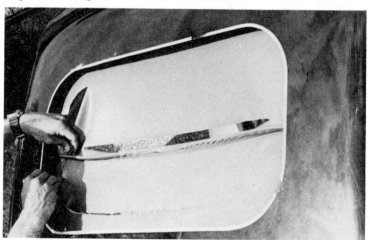
Fig. 4-13. Cutting the headliner.

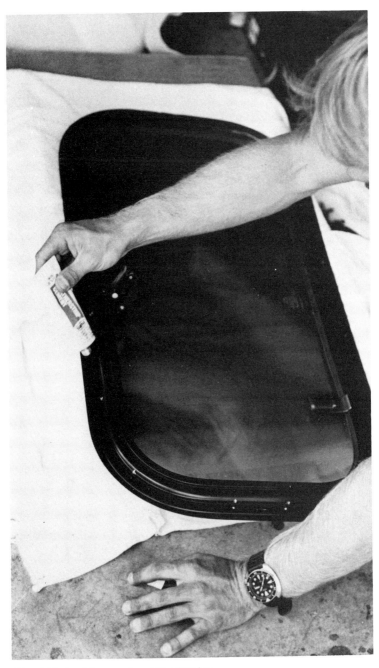

Fig. 4-14. Applying weatherstrip adhesive.

Fig. 4-15. Placing sealant material.

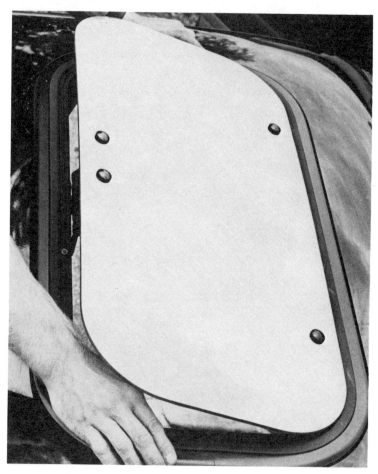
Fig. 4-16. Inserting sunroof section.

58

Fig. 4-17. Securing trim ring.

Fig. 4-18. Weather sealant excess.

of the sunroof frame squeeze together against the roof skin, compressing and expanding the sealer material. This consequently weather strips and seals the outer edges. The sealant material will tend to ooze out past the edge of the frame (Fig. 4-18) after tightening. This excess is trimmed away and discarded. In time, this ooz-

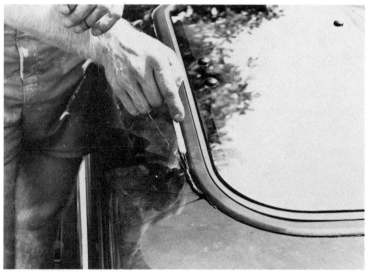

Fig. 4-19. Removing excess sealant.

ing process may continue and future removal may be required (Fig. 4-19).

Installing this type of sunroof does not require much expertise or tooling. It can be undertaken by even the neophyte, if suggestions and instructions are followed exactly.

Chapter 5

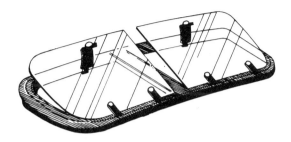

T-top Installation

The T-top is a highly stylish, sporty additive that is the most distinguished, as well as distinctive, of all the sunroof types. Though not a sunroof in every sense of the word, it does have features in common with the sunroof category.

When it is installed, the T-top immediately becomes a permanent entity of the car itself, radically changing the visual and structural aspects of the car. This face-lifting modifies, if not the overcall, then at least the roof lines, improving the appearance.

Figures 5-1 and 5-2 show the Chrysler Le Baron and Chevy Monte Carlo, respectively, sporting Cars & Concepts sunroofs. The distinctive, upgraded look has made Cars & Concepts sunroofs very popular aftermarket customizing accessories. Many dealers have them installed on select showroom vehicles to boost consumer interest and sales.

The T-roof has many exclusive and patented features that make it a sound unit that proves the infallibility of additive T-top installation. The full glass-to-glass panels on most T-tops help to preserve, as well as enhance, the overall roof line while offering optimum ventilation facilities. Whether for comfort or styling, the T-top is here to stay judging by its widespread popularity.

SUPPLIERS

Two companies have come to the fore in providing T-tops for

Fig. 5-1. An '82 LeBaron with a C & C T-top treatment. Courtesy Cars & Concepts.

Fig. 5-2. Monte Carlo T-top elegance. Courtesy Cars & Concepts.

the consumer, dealer, and aftermarket. They are Cars & Concepts and Pacific. Both are mass producers and distributors of T-tops for the more popular cars of today.

The Cars & Concepts Skylite is presently available for automobile models as follows:

- ☐ 1973-1984 Chevrolet Camaro (available in black finish only)
- ☐ 1973-1984 Pontiac Firebird (available in black finish only)
- ☐ 1978-1984 Chevrolet Monte Carlo
- ☐ 1978-1984 Oldsmobile Cutlass
- ☐ 1978-1984 Buick Regal
- ☐ 1978-1984 Pontiac Grand Prix
- ☐ 1977-1980 Dodge Aspen
- ☐ 1977-1980 Plymouth Volare
- ☐ 1980-1984 Dodge Mirada
- ☐ 1980-1984 Chrysler Cordoba
- ☐ 1979-1984 Ford Mustang (2-door and 3-door)
- ☐ 1979-1984 Mercury Capri (3-door)

All Cars & Concepts products have a 12-month or 12,000-mile warranty and are backed by international dealer network.

While Cars & Concepts has the domestic market pretty well covered, Pacific offers excellent T-tops for the Japanese imports. Late model Datsuns, Toyota Celicas, and Supras may now sport Pacific T-tops specifically designed for those late-model cars. They feature special Solarcool tempered PPG tinted glass and easy lift panels. Included in the package (as in all T-top packages) are soft vinyl covers to protect the glass panels when they are stored away.

INSTALLATION

Regardless of the type or manufacturer, T-tops are in no way consumer do-it-yourself installation items. Before a T-top is installed, the roof must undergo radical surgery. In fact a greater part of the roof section, starting about 5 inches back from the windshield to the back door frame, must be removed. It must be cut away precisely with no margin for error. Next, the roof area must be reinforced, then modified to accommodate the T-top panels.

The important structural piece that serves to make this all possible is the one-piece, H-shaped heavy steel frame assembly (see Fig. 5-3). This durable frame has a dual purpose: it strengthens and unifies the roof and, when installed, becomes the frame housing for

Fig. 5-3. Larry Moffo of Sunroofs of Florida exhibits the Cars & Concepts
stamped steel frame assembly.

67

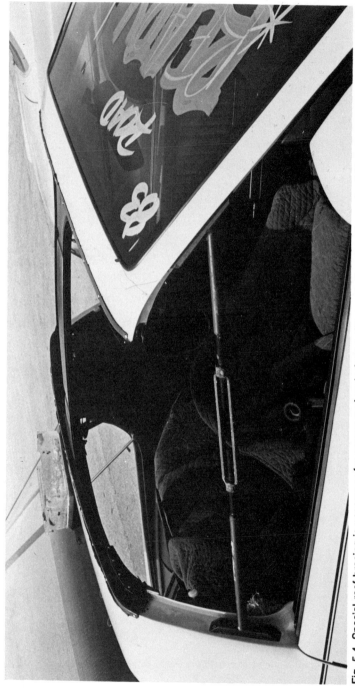

Fig. 5-4. Special roof bracing is necessary for proper roof main frame alignment. Courtesy Sunroofs of Florida.

Fig. 5-5. Steel frame is rigidly secured. Courtesy Sunroofs of Florida.

the T-top panels. Since the roof is considerably weakened when sectioned, side bracing must be applied. It spaces and secures the remaining cut roof sections before the T-top frame brace is mounted (Fig. 5-4). As the brace performs its function, the frame piece (or roof backbone) is permanently and positively affixed by riveting (Fig.

Fig. 5-6. The root T-top frame in place. Trim is added to finalize and hide rivet heads. Courtesy Sunroofs of Florida.

5-5). Figure 5-6 shows the main frame fully secured. All that remains is the addition of edge molding which will hide the unsightly securing elements while enhancing decor. Once the backbone frame installation is finished, the T-tops can be easily fitted into place.

You can see in the photos the complexity and exacting work involved in an installation of this type. If mounting specifications are not rigidly followed, a car can be ruined. It would then require excessive body work to bring it back to normal. One can easily realize why T-top manufacturers and outlets stress professional installation and will not sell to parties other than T-top facilities or qualified auto body shops.

If T-tops are for you, we strongly suggest going the acknowledged route—via your local T-top representative. More information on T-tops can be found in Chapter 2, Manufacturers and Suppliers.

Chapter 6

Sunroofs in Vans, Trucks, and Off-Road Vehicles

In autos and sports cars, sunroofs serve a primary function as custom, luxury, aesthetic additives. The same can be said for vans, but with an added factor—ventilation.

VANS

The van originally designed as a commercial vehicle was not designed along cruising comfort lines. Air-conditioning is an optional feature, but vans without it require better air flow for passenger comfort, particularly in hot weather. Because a van sunroof can do much to enhance overall ventilation, it is a common and desired accessory and an attractive one at that. It improves the exterior look of the van, while increasing driver and passenger comfort.

Van sunroofs are generally larger than their automobile counterparts. They can afford to be because vans sport a greater roof area both back to front and, of more importance, in width.

A typical example is this top-of-the-line Stretch Forming van sunroof (Fig. 6-1). Designed for the newer Ford vans, it measures 17″ × 35″. The Ford van roof contains a series of protruding ribs running from front to back. For this reason the Stretch Forming frame contains a series of convex dimples to accommodate the roof rib factor. It allows the sunroof a conforming fit when placed on the roof (Fig. 6-2). This is a desirable feature for Ford owners. Other van sunroofs in the company line offer similar custom-contoured fitting.

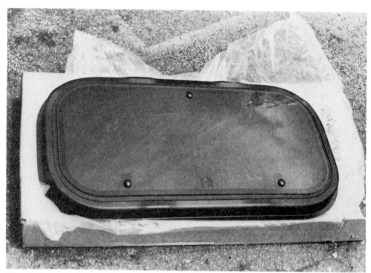

Fig. 6-1. Stretch Forming sunroof for Ford Econoline Van.

Another common popular setup for vans is utilizing two sunroofs: one in front and one in back (fig. 6-3). This Chevy van features two Hammond sunroofs, one over the driver's compartment and one set to the rear of the roof. The logic behind this is shown in Fig. 6-4. A continuous flow of air is initiated by the insertion of two sunroofs (A and B) in the roof. Air flows over the top of the

Fig. 6-2. Indentations in Stretch Forming frame to accommodate roof ribs.

Fig. 6-3. Chevy van with two sunroofs.

van as it is in motion, with a small amount of this slipstream entering the front sunroof. In addition, air flows through the front side windows and into the van (dotted arrows) creating a continuous flow to the rear of the van where some of the air exits through the rear sunroof. This configuration offers optimum ventilation and continuous air flow while the van is in motion.

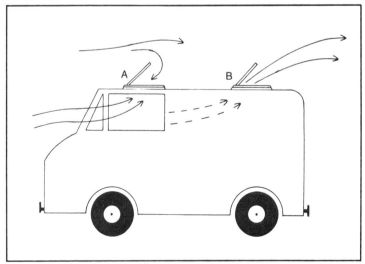

Fig. 6-4. Air flow in a van with dual sunroof installation.

This front intake-rear exhaust setup is very popular in larger vehicles. For this reason there are also roof vents and exhaust vents manufactured to be used to stimulate air exhaust and air flow that work in unison with front-mounted sunroofs. When the sunroofs and side windows are in a maximum open position, note how much volumetric area is viable to air entering the van.

One does not necessarily have to go the dual sunroof route for upgraded ventilation. A number of vents are marketed for rear roof positioning that take up less room, yet stimulate air flow and exhaust equally well in place of a second sunroof.

Figure 6-5 shows a Hammond Vanvent being installed in a van roof. The overall dimensions of the Hammond Vanvent is 14" × 14" with 4-inch radius corners. Color options include translucent white, smoke, and blue. The Vanvent opens frontward or rearward. It contains a two-speed fan which, at its top speed, exhausts 350 cubic feet a minute. The Vanvent is an easy to install as a sunroof. The Econovent (Fig. 6-6) is a nonpowered (sans fan), more moderately priced, version of the Hammond Vanvent. An even more compact, less obtrusive, but highly efficient unit is marketed by

Fig. 6-5. Hammond Vanvent in process of installation. Vent is clip-secured from inside the van.

Fig. 6-6. The Econovent by Hammond.

Hammond called the Roof Blower (Fig. 6-7). This smaller unit will mount in a 6-inch diameter hole and will exhaust air at 90 cubic feet per minute. Other Hammond sunroofs and accessories are presented in Chapter 2, Manufacturers and Suppliers.

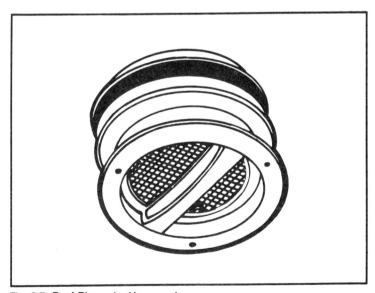

Fig. 6-7. Roof Blower by Hammond.

Fig. 6-8. Custom Ford Bronco.

BRONCOS AND BLAZERS

The Ford Bronco and Chevy Blazer, modern counterparts of the station wagon, also take to sunroof installation. Figure 6-8 shows an older Ford Bronco customized and upgraded with the addition of a cab-mounted sunroof. Midroof sunroof installation is also feasi-

Fig. 6-9. Sunroof also improves interior aspects of the Bronco. Courtesy Jim Wimpy.

Fig. 6-10. Small Stretch Forming sunroof in Luv Pickup.

ble, but for aesthetic reasons it is better to install it in the cab area (Fig. 6-9) where it also serves as interior enhancement.

PICKUPS AND OFF-ROAD VEHICLES

The pickup cab will benefit from a sunroof installation which

Fig. 6-11. Off-road rig and sunroof. Courtesy Gold Coast Truck Sales, Lighthouse Point, FL.

Fig. 6-12. Closeup of dual sunroof in off-road Toyota, 4-wheel drive. Courtesy Gold Coast Truck Sales.

adds a sporty look to the work vehicle while upgrading ventilation. Fig. 6-10 shows a small one-piece Stretch Forming model housed in the cab of the Chevy Luv pickup.

Figure 6-11 shows a Toyota 4-wheel drive pickup typically set up in off-road regalia. The two-piece sunroof unit adds to the overall appearance of this uniquely styled vehicle and allows more light and air to enter the cab while the vehicle is in motion. Figure 6-12 shows a close-up view of the sunroof in the cab roof with one of the dual sections open.

You can see now how even mundane vehicles can be glamorized with the addition of a sunroof. In all cases driver comfort can be upgraded with the increased air intake it allows.

Chapter 7

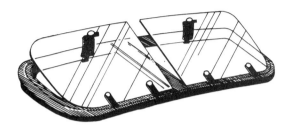

Electric Sunroofs

By far, the most sophisticated, opulent, desirable, and most highly functional sunroofs are the electric or powered models which offer complete control at the touch of a button. There are a few electric sunroof manufacturers. They two most worthy of note are Hollandia and American Sunroof. The currently offer national facilities for sunroof installation through designated outlets.

AMERICAN SUNROOFS

American Sunroof, based in Los Angeles, markets two formidable sunroof units: the Sungazer and the Stargazer. The Sungazer is a strong and durable metal panel sunroof that opens up at the touch of a switch. It is basically a highly efficient ventilating unit that can be fully or partly opened as desired. As a decor additive, the Sungazer incorporates an arrodized aluminum peripheral molding and outside edging.

The Stargazer model is identical to the Sungazer in every respect save for a reflective glass opening panel that it has in place of the metal one. Closed, it allows extra light to enter the driving compartment. Open, it affords maximum ventilation. Two glass color options are featured: silver or gold. An integrated sunshade to close off the roof opening entirely is also included in the Stargazer package. Figure 7-1 shows the American Sunroof Stargazer model. The smooth lines of the unit blend in well with the roof surface.

Fig. 7-1. The American Electric Sunroof.

Figure 7-2 shows the Stargazer in a partially open position and Fig. 7-3 the same unit in a fully open mode.

Neither of the American Sunroof offerings are recommended for do-it-yourself installation, nor is any electric unit for that matter. The installer *must* have sophisticated equipment plus above average skills and mechanical ability. First, the units are bulky. Ex-

Fig. 7-2. American Sunroof partially opened.

Fig. 7-3. American Sunroof fully opened.

acting installation and fit are mandatory for proper insertion of the sunroof and mechanism into the roof cutout, which must also be cut to stringent specifications. Figure 7-4 shows the American Sunroof, motor, and frame assembly prior to installation.

Figures 7-5 through 7-10 were taken at Sunroofs of Florida (Ft.

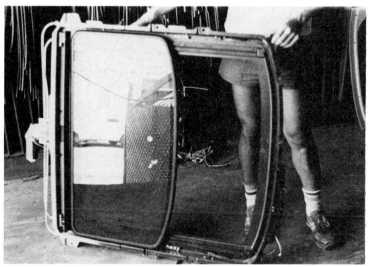

Fig. 7-4. The complete American Sunroof unit and frame. Courtesy Sunroofs of Florida.

Fig. 7-5. For proper roof cutting, a power saw unit is necessary. Courtesy Sunroofs of Florida.

Lauderdale, Florida), a leading sunroof installation facility and outlet for American Sunroof. They illustrate the proper and exacting procedures so critical in modular electric sunroof installation.

First an opening must be cut into the roof. Since there is little margin for error in this initial step, sophisticated cutting equipment, such as this ceiling-hung, heavy-duty carbide blade, are almost mandatory in order to do the job correctly and professionally (Fig. 7-5). In Fig. 7-6 we see the critical and precise opening realized with the commercial power saw. The taped template assists in centering and locating the sunroof cutout area. The garnish ring and frame for the sunroof go in next (Fig. 7-7). Interior design must be considered, so to embellish the inner decor and the sunroof on the headliner side, a specially designed inner frame piece is utilized (Fig. 7-8). Figure 7-9 shows the inside trim frame installed. Powering the American Sunroof is a handy, powerful, and highly efficient motor (Fig. 7-10).

HOLLANDIA SUNROOFS

Hollandia-Sunroofs Inc. is a U.S. subsidiary of the world's oldest designer and innovator of automotive sunroofs located in the city of Haarlem in the Netherlands (Holland). The parent company, now enjoying its 85th year in business, specialized in its formative years

Fig. 7-6. The opening for the American Sunroof. Note how the template aids in proper size conformation.

Fig. 7-7. Garnish ring installed.

in custom building for the automotive and truck trade. Aftermarket products soon became a mainstay of the production curriculum. Vermeulen-Hollandia B.V. of the Netherlands obtained its first worldwide sunroof patent in 1936 and currently supplies 22 countries from its three Dutch and Belgian factories.

The quality of Hollandia is so well recognized that the company

Fig. 7-8. Inside headliner trim-ring. Courtesy American Sunroof.

Fig. 7-9. American Sunroof unit and interior trim headliner installed.

has won OEM contracts to supply sliding sunroofs to such leading European automobile manufacturers as Fiat, Jaguar, Saab, Rover, Honda of Britain, and Mazda of Germany. In addition Rolls-Royce unofficially recommends the Hollandia flush-fitting sliding roofs.

Hollandia offers basically two ultrasophisticated design types: the Electric Glass Sliding roof and another model type designated

Fig. 7-10. American motor drive unit.

the Sun-Slider. The Electric Glass Sliding roofs were made with rotary screw-drive, and a newer designed Model 61 offers an internal cable-drive mechanism specially designed for small U.S. and import cars.

The acclaimed Hollandia sunroofs offer many distinctive, innovative, and preferred features. They have the thinnest housings which provide the least loss of headroom. The Sun-Slider model has a patented wind deflector which substantially reduces wind noise. The two motive drives for the Glass Slider model are functionally perfect; the rigid worm-screw type in the larger and stan-

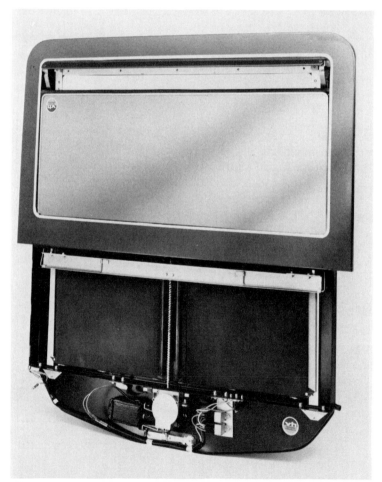

Fig. 7-11. Hollandia Streamline Sunroof kit. Note worm-drive motor mechanism. Courtesy Hollandia.

dard Glass Slider versions, and the cable (trunk-mounted type) for the smaller import and similar vehicles. Figure 7-11 shows the Standard Streamline Glass Slider rotary-worm drive model in its entirety. The unit and its drive mechanism is extremely well designed, making it easy to service as well as install.

Other Hollandia features include stainless steel adjustable trimrings; one-way, mirror-type shatterproof glass; interchangeable steel and glass panels; built-in power safety and overload cut-off mechanism; super quiet motor drives; prewired, plug-in electric circuits; drain tubes, emergency operating ratchet, and all installation parts for each installation kit. A range of sizes is shown in Table 7-1.

Table 7-1. Hollandia Sliding Roof Sizes.

Electric Quick-Fit Roofs	Panel Length × Panel Width
Electric Sun-SlidersTS17″ × 33″	
Electric Steel-Top Roofs	
Model 81	17″ × 32 1/4″
Model 82	17″ × 35 1/2″
Model 85	17″ × 35 1/2″
Model 87	17″ × 39″
Model 88	19″ × 39″
Electric Glass-Top Roofs	
Model 71	17″ × 32 1/4″
Model 72	17″ × 35 1/2″
Model 77	17″ × 39″
Model 79	21″ × 39″
Model 61 Trunk-Mounted Motor	17″ × 32 1/4″

Flanging bar and template for Model 71 will also install Models 81 and 61.
Flanging bar and template for Model 72 will also install Model 82.
Flanging bar and template for Model 77 will also install Model 87.

Each Hollandia installer has been furnished with a detailed sliding roof application guide list. Almost every imported and domestic automobile is listed in the guide. All available Hollandia Electric Sliding Roof models are listed in Table 7-2 along with their applications.

Table 7-2. Hollandia Sliding Roof Application Chart.

For a quick reference, we are listing all available Hollandia Electric sliding roof models with their general application:

Model 81	Electric Steel	
Model 71	Electric Glass	Alfa Romeo, B.M.W., Datsun, Honda, Mazda, Subaru, Toyota, Volkswagen, Volvo, Chevette, Sunbird, Bobcat, Pinto, Mustang, K-Cars, Aspen, Omni, Horizon, Champ, Spirit, Fiesta, Escort.
Model 82	Electric Steel	
Model 72	Electric Glass	F-bodies, A-bodies, X-bodies, Seville, Toronado, Eldorado, Le Baron, Cordoba, Volare, Concord, Monarch, Zephyr, L.T.D., Fairmont, Granada, Volvo, Toyota, Jaguar, Mazda, Alfa Romeo, Mercedes, Bentlye.
Model 87	Electric Steel	
Model 77	Electric Glass	Peugot-604, Rover, Mercedes, A-Body Wagons, A-Body Landau Models.
Model 88	Electric Steel	
Model 79	Electric Glass	Electra, Le Sabre, Fleetwood, Coupe de Ville, Sedan De Ville, 98 Regency, Bonneville, Catalina, Continental Mark VI, Lincoln Continental, L.T.D., New Yorker.
Model	Sun-Slider	Fits the smallest car and upwards to the A-body size automobiles.

Installers are responsible for checking the proper measurements of each type and model car to be worked on. Request Hollandia's assistance if in doubt.

Fig. 7-12. Hollandia Streamline Glass Sunroof. Courtesy Hollandia.

HOLLANDIA ELECTRIC SUNROOFS

Though there are options offered with the Hollandia Sunroofs, there are basically two types marketed by this company. Both are superior, magnificent offerings that have helped fortify the excellent second-to-none Hollandia reputation.

The more conventional standard electric sunroof is the Streamline Sliding Sunroof. Figures 7-12 and 7-13 show the Streamline Glass Slider; Fig. 7-12 in the closed position, Fig. 7-13

Fig. 7-13. Hollandia Streamline in open position. Courtesy Hollandia.

Fig. 7-14. Interior view Hollandia headliner adaptation. Courtesy Hollandia.

in the open position. In Fig. 7-14 we can study this sunroof from the interior of the car, noting the excellent aesthetic qualities that make it look as if it was specially designed for optimum headliner enhancement. Figure 7-15 shows another view of the headliner interior treatment. The Hollandia Quick-Fit Streamline Sliding Roof models are universal and applicable to most current model automobiles.

Included in Table 7-3, is a reprint of Hollandia's Technical Bulletin #76, which should help as a guide to size and model selection. This bulletin encompasses Hollandia 70 and 80 series model sunroofs.

For further assisting the prospective buyer, Table 7-4 is a listing from Hollandia's Technical Bulletin #81. It provides added information on placement of the Streamline Slider in current automobile models, giving the proper front distance measurements and interior modification recommendations.

HOLLANDIA STREAMLINE GLASS SLIDER MOTOR DRIVES

Opening and closing of the Streamline Slider Sunroof panel is governed by a powerful motor mounted internally in the rearmost portion of the sunroof housing. This strong, highly reliable motor unit turns a screw-worm gear (of shaft) which, as it revolves, advances or retracts the sliding sunroof panel. This motor mechanism configuration may be seen in Fig. 7-11.

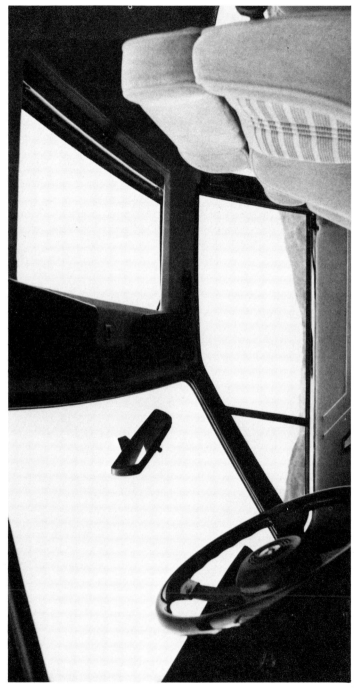

Fig. 7-15. Side view interior Hollandia installation. Courtesy Hollandia.

Table 7-3. Hollandia's Technical Bulletin #76.

```
TECHNICAL BULLETIN  NO. 76
---------------------------

This technical bulletin is to be used as a guide only.Installers
are responsible for checking the proper measurements of each type
and model car to be worked on.

Make sure,that the inner (lower) flanging bar fits properly on the
inside of the roof before cutting the hole.Also check the lenght of
the roof kit against the lenght of the inside roof.

If not sure about the front distance of the cut-out,the sunvisors
might be of help. The front cut-out line should be a ¼ inch behind
the sunvisors when same are in rest position.

Installers are kindly requested to advise Hollandia of any required
changes in this list and Hollandia will appriciate additional data
such as front distance and unusual situations you may encounter.

REMARKS:
----------

             - In some cases front distance has not been recorded.

             - Abbreviations used: FD = Front distance in CM.

                                   HA = Manual

                                   EL = Electric

                                   GT = Glass-Top

                                   SL = Streamline/Quick-fit

                 --------------O------------


HOLLANDIA'S RANGE OF SLIDING ROOFS AVAILABLE FROM U.S. STOCK
------------------------------------------------------------

MANUAL STEEL SLIDING ROOFS          PANEL LENGHT     PANEL WIDTH
                          ____                      ____

MODEL   50.....................     15  inch    X   32   inch
MODEL   51.....................     19¼ inch    X   32¼ inch

ELECT. STEEL SLIDING ROOFS
                          ____

MODEL   81.....................     17  inch    X   32¼ inch
MODEL   82.....................     17  inch    X   35½ inch
MODEL   85.....................     17  inch    X   35½ inch
MODEL   87.....................     17  inch    X   39   inch
MODEL   88.....................     19  inch    X   39   inch

GLASS-TOP   SLIDING ROOFS
                          ____

MODEL 71.......................     17  inch    X   32¼ inch
MODEL 72.......................     17  inch    X   35½ inch
MODEL 77.......................     17  inch    X   39   inch
MODEL 79.......................     21  inch    X   39   inch

QUICK-FIT   SLIDING ROOFS
                          ____

MODEL SL.......................     19¼ inch    X   32½ inch

        Flanging bars and templates for the steel electric
        roofs 81-82 and 87 have the exact same measurements
        and can also be used to install the electric glass-
        top models 71-72 and 77.

                 =========O===========
```

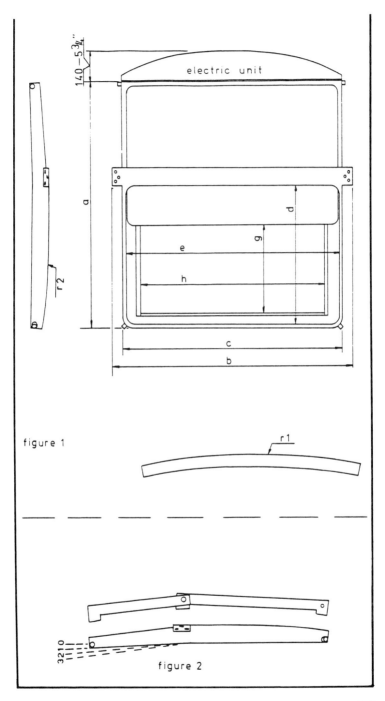

electric unit

figure 1

figure 2

95

Table 7-3. Continued.

DIMENSIONS OF THE HOUSING FRAMES

ROOF CODE	A INCH	B INCH	C INCH	D INCH	E INCH	G INCH	H INCH	CURVERTURE CODE
MANUAL KITS								R1- R2
50	26 3/4	36½	33	15	32½	8¼	27½	28-22
51	36 ½	36½	33	19 3/4	32¼	13¼	27½	28-62
ELECT. KITS								
81	33 3/4	36½	33	17	32¼	13¼	27½	28-22
82	33 3/4	39 3/4	36¼	17	35½	13¼	30 3/4	64-22
BMW. 83	30 3/4	39 3/4	36¼	15½	35½	11½	30 3/4	64-22
87	33 3/4	43¼	39 3/4	17	39	13¼	34¼	82-22
88	37 3/4	43¼	39 3/4	19	39	15¼	34¼	82-22
GLASS TOP KITS								
71	33 3/4	36½	33	17	32¼	13¼	27½	28-22
72	33 3/4	39 3/4	36¼	17	35½	13¼	30 3/4	64-22
77	33 3/4	43¼	39 3/4	17	39	13¼	34¼	82-22
79	41 3/4	43¼	39 3/4	21	39	17¼	34¼	82-72

The cross and side gauge that you will receive with a standard tool set, measures the FRONT PART of the housing frame.(r 1 and 2 on figure)

The rear part of the housing frame should be adjusted to the curverture of the car roof with the help of the hinging side gauge (figure 2)

Table 7-4. Hollandia's Technical Bulletin #81. (Continued through page 101.)

Placement of Streamline Slider

	Front distance cm.	Remarks
Alfa Romeo		
Alfasud	19	Replace interior light
AMC		
Pacer/Pacer Station wagon	22	Change left corner molding
Audi		
50	22	
80	22	
Austin		
Allegro 1100	20	
Maxi 1750	21	
Princess	21	
Autobianchi		
A 112	18	New headlining
BMW		
1502 until 2002	20	
316/318/320	19	Replace interior light
Chrysler		
160 B 2 ltr.	20	
Avenger (4-d)	20	
Citroen		
LN	17	New headlining; replace interior light
Ami 8	26	Replace interior light
GS Special	22	Replace interior light
GS Club	22	Replace interior light
GS X2	22	Replace interior light
Visa	21	New headlining

	Front distance cm.	Remarks
Daihatsu		
Charmant	22	
Cuore		
Datsun		
120 Y	20	Replace interior light
120 Y coupe	16	Modify rear retainer strip (part no. 2, expl. view 750925001); replace interior light
Cherry '79	20	
Sunny 140Y	22	
160/180 series		New headlining
Laurel (200 l.)		
Fiat		
124	20	
126	18	New headlining
127	19	
128 N	19	
128, 128 3 p.	19	
133	18	New headlining
Ford		
Escort	19	
Escort 1300 Sport	19	
Taunus	21	
Capri	19	
Fiesta	21	
Honda		

Civic	22	
Accord	22	
Lada		
1200 until 1600	20 or 30	
Lancia		
H.P.E.	22	
Mazda		
1000, 1300	21	
323 series	22	
818	19	
616 special	21	
121 L.		
626	18	
Mini		
850		
Cooper	21	
Clubman	22	
Estate	21	Fasten interior lining with screws
Mitsubishi	22	Fasten interior lining with screws
Lancer	19	
Sigma	19	New headlining
Galant Sigma	20	New headlining
Colt 2 d.	21	
Morris		
Marina	21	
Opel		
Kadett City series	19	
Kadett series (excl. coupe)	19	

	Front distance cm.	Remarks
Ascona series	19	
Rekord series 1978	22	
Commodore	22	
Peugeot		
104 GL/SL	20	Bend rear roof stiffening
304 series	18	
504 excl. coupe	26	
Renault		
4	14	New headlining
5	21	New headlining
6	17	
12	16	
14	21	New headlining
15	16	
16	17	
18	21	
Simca		
1005/1006	23	
Ralley	23	
1100 series	21	
1307, 1308 series	22	New headlining
Horizon	18	New headlining
Skoda		
105/120 series	20	
Subaru		
1400 series (excl. coupe)	19	
Custom		
Toyota		

Model		Remarks
1000 special series	19	New headlining
Corolla 30-series (1978 model)	20	New headlining, replace interior light
Tercel	22	
Carina-series	23	New headlining, replace interior light
Corona Mk 2	18	
Starlett		
Triumph		
Dolomite	23	
Vauxhall		
Chevette	18	
Cavalier	18	
Royale		
Volkswagen		
Golf	22	
Polo	19	
Scirocco	18	
Passat	22	
Volvo		
66 series	18	
343 series	23	
Zastava		
1100	18	

General remarks: When installing into station cars, avoid dimpling the car roof at the rear corners.

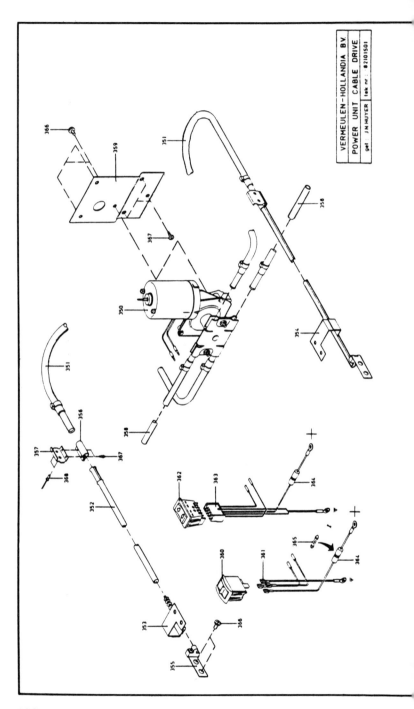

VERMEULEN-HOLLANDIA BV

POWER UNIT CABLE DRIVE

get J.N.HUYER tek nr : 82101501

102

PARTSLIST.

Power unit cable drive drawing nr. 821010501.

Pos.	Description	Numb.
350	Motor Lucas	1
351	Extension tube	2
352	Drive tube	2
353	Drive cable (Rh)	1
354	Drive cable (Lh)	1
355	Front mounting bracket	2
356	Tube holder	2
357	Rear mounting bracket	2
358	Store tube	2
359	Motor mounting bracket	1
360	Switch model 1	1
361	Wire harness model 1	1
362	Switch model 2	1
363	Wire harness model 2	1
364	Fuse holder	1
365	Fuse 15 Amp.	1
366	M5 × 10 kombiscrew	7
367	Parkerscrew AB 6 × 3/8 PH Phillips head	7
368	Poprivet 3, 2 × 8 alum.	4

Fig. 7-16. Power unit cable-drive mechanism drawing. Courtesy Hollandia.

The most recent addition to the Hollandia Streamline Sun-Slider roster is the Model 61, designed to allow trunk installation of the control motor. In the Model 61 unit, the glass panel is guided by a cable on each side serving to drive the sliding arms. The use of the 17″ × 33″ glass panel results in extremely smooth opening and closing and avoids the "jerky" movements often attributed to single center-cable drive systems.

The motor unit for the Model 61, produced by Lucas of England, is the same highly efficient, low-noise unit used extensively by many European car makers. Figure 7-16, a reprint from Hollandia's Model 61 bulletin, illustrates the motor drive unit and its integral functional parts.

According to Martin Pot, President of Hollandia-Sunroofs Inc. of Eden Prairie, Minnesota, the newest Model 61 cable-drive Sunroof was introduced to meet the sunroof installation requirements of such cars as the Chevy Camaro, Pontiac Firebird, Toyota Supra and Celica, Dodge Challenger, and other similar automobiles. With its drain pan size of 34 inches (length) and 33 inches (width), it also fits many of the "bubble back" cars first introduced in 1983. The Model 61 Cable-Drive Sunroof fits flush with the car roof. It contains a stainless steel trim-ring around the roof opening edge plus a self-storing wind deflector. The unit is priced in line with the other four Hollandia Streamline spindle-drive sunroofs.

HOLLANDIA SUN-SLIDER

In keeping with current avant-garde designs, Hollandia recently introduced its novel Sun-Slider. Originally introduced in Europe a few years ago, the Sun-Slider immediately gained wide acceptance in the automotive field. The revolutionary new design was so well received that Fiat of Italy features the Sun-Slider as original equipment on many of its passenger cars.

The major advantages of the unit also offered to the American market include an attractively designed, full-glass top measuring 17″ × 33″. As the glass top opens, it tilts upward, which is another welcomed feature. The engineered frame incorporates an almost universal curvature, allowing it to flush fit on nearly all U.S. and foreign automobiles. The moving glass panel, which opens to the degree desired both in the front and rear, is designed with a spoiler effect to maximize airflow while keeping wind noise at a minimal level. Water buildup is effectively controlled by means of front drain tubes. The roof frame is solidly constructed of sturdy aluminum with moving parts of stainless steel.

Another major advantage of the Sun-Slider is a conveniently installed control button situated in an attractive overhead console that also upgrades interior headliner decor. Offered also is an optional wind deflector that keeps wind and rain out of the driving compartment even at slow driving speeds. The wind deflector with its smoky tint matches the sunroof glass color and may be permanently mounted across the front edges of the sunroof.

The attractively designed Sun-Slider is presented in Fig. 7-17. Included also in this photo is the front-mounted wind deflector, a highly recommended option that upgrades the functional aspects of this sunroof. Figure 7-18 illustrates the interior styling and operative console of the Sun-Slider, the motor activated by the simple touch of a button.

Those interested in Hollandia sunroofs will find that a do-it-yourself approach is out of the questions (as in the case with T-tops). The Hollandia distributorship does not recommend, condone, or even make possible the acquisition of its sunroofs or parts to the general public. Hollandia will not make available sunroof kits or components to second or third parties. The Hollandia line must be purchased and installed by knowledgeable, authorized dealers of which there are many throughout the country.

The reasoning behind this is justifiable. An electric sunroof installation is far more complicated than a simple pop-in, one-piece sunroof insertion, such as described in Chapter 4. For one thing the

Fig. 7-17. Hollandia Sun-Slider Model in open position. This illustration also shows optional front wind deflector unit.

Fig. 7-18. Sun-Slider pushbutton console operation.

car roof must be cut open, and the machine work is critical with no margin for error (see Fig. 7-19). A special cutting shear is recommended, and in many cases, the operation must be performed by two people. Another person should hold the metal steady as it is cut to minimize vibration of the sheet metal which can effect precise manipulation of the cutting shears. After cutting, all edges must be filed and ground smooth and evenly, a tedious task with no short cuts allowed. Secondly, certain flanging bars must be utilized and perfectly aligned before the sunroof unit is mounted. In most cases this requires specialized tooling accessible to Hollandia installation facilities.

If you are considering the purchase and installation of an electric sunroof, it is wise and mandatory that the operation be done by a knowledgeable dealer authorized to provide the unit of your choice.

Fig. 7-19. Cutting the roof for electric sunroof installation is an exacting and tedious operation.

107

Chapter 8

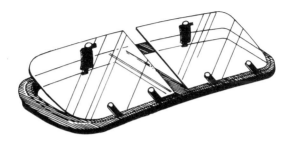

Custom Sunroofs

Though sunroofs are approached as functional features by some people they can also serve as custom additives. They can add to the overall sportiness of a vehicle or become an integral part of the aesthetic design of the car. In some instances, the sunroof can become one of the focal points of the car, particular in a custom car situation.

THE "VETTERFLY"

A typical example is the custom Corvette featured in Fig. 8-1 in which the sunroof is a part of the customizing theme while also enhancing the decor. This show-winning 1975 Corvette is owned and exhibited frequently by its creators, Ron and Carlotta De Lucia of North Miami. Ron, a custom entrepreneur and Corvette expert, owns and operates the most exclusive Corvette repair and detailing shop in the Miami area. His custom excellence has been featured in many of the leading automotive publications in the country generating much acclaim for the "Corvette Specialists" shop and Ron's creative expertise.

The "Vetterfly" itself is owned by Ron's wife, Carlotta. Though originally a stock version it was literally rebuilt from the ground up—redesigned, restyled, and in all aspects, improved upon. The 'vette was conceived around a butterfly theme. Construction begun on the car's center section, progressing to the front back. The cen-

Fig. 8-1. The "Vetterfly" Custom Sunroof.

tral focal point is the butterfly sunroof which dominates the car and puts a heavy emphasis on the "butterfly" theme.

The sunroof section started out as a one-piece transparent section (or a one-piece T-top) once marketed on a wide scale by Corvette accessory manufacturers. Originally the car was structured to house standard dual T-tops, then with minor modifications re-

Fig. 8-2. Specially designed block-mounts for custom roof.

Fig. 8-3. Interior view, Vetterfly sunroof.

styled to accommodate the one-piece clear sunroof. In Fig. 8-1 we see the butterfly one-piece T-top section in place.

Holding the roof section firmly in place are plastic foundation mounts permanently secured to the roof-sunroof section (Fig. 8-2). Four of these circular block mounts are located along the central portion of the roof section which line up to accommodating brackets that bolt up against the mounting blocks. Figure 8-3 shows the mounting block-bracket mounts and how they secure to the central T-post, which is a part of the roof frame structure. The mount and block setup is strategically placed so that when the sunroof section is in place, the overall fit is exact and secure.

Situating the butterfly silhouette onto the tinted see-through part required a little work based on clever ingenuity. First the butterfly silhouette was laid out in 1/8-inch masking tape for the overall design. The butterfly section was filled in with masking tape and masking paper to protect and cover the butterfly silhouette surface. The rest of the sunroof area was then liberally painted with acrylic lacquer, the same color as the overall base color of the car. Masking was then removed leaving the butterfly silhouette and creating the highly unusualy sunroof effect. Figure 8-4 shows the roof section removed. Note the exacting symmetry and formidable design work which makes this roof stand out among all others.

Carrying on the butterfly theme are the taillights. These were

Fig. 8-4. Ron De Lucia and the one-piece glamorized sunroof.

Fig. 8-5. Taillights repeat butterfly sunroof theme.

hand-cut from fiberglass with hand-shaped, red plastic lenses set into place (Fig. 8-5).

Untold hours of refined custom work went into the rest of the fabrication on this unique vehicle. Integrated into the front end are modified Eckler custom fiberglass additives, such as a fiberglass replacement hood and spoiler. Twelve yards of Cherise velour grace the interior upholstery as well as twelve yards of matching deep pile shag carpeting. Mild flaring was added to the front and rear wheel walls to accommodate the wide tread tires and custom wheels.

The overall car sports many coats of Metalflake Heather Pearl paint laid on flawlessly by Ron himself. The murals and artistic effects echoing the butterfly theme were administered by Debra Simpson (a.k.a. Sliique), a prominent south Florida and California muralist.

All the extra custom additives, components, and artwork involved set off this creation of customizing excellence. The vehicle is a prime example of the impact a properly designed and implemented sunroof can have on a finely styled showpiece. Ron De Lucia's "Veterfly" has taken top trophy honors in custom shows, sweeping such categories as "Best Late Model Custom," "Most Outstanding Hand-Built Radical Custom," "People's Choice," and "Best Overall."

OTHER CUSTOM LOOKS

Another custom example, this time using a simple popped-in

Fig. 8-6. Sunroof and overhead console combo creates great custom interior look. Vehicle designed by Terry Short.

Fig. 8-7. Cars & Concepts T-top in custom Trans Am.

sunroof, is presented in Fig. 8-6 showing the interior of a Chevy "EL Camino." Here a Dual Sunroof was inserted into the frontal roof section of the Camino. As a custom additive, this unit not only adds to the overall exterior facade of the car, but also allows natural light to illuminate the overhead console unit containing CB and stereo components. It also provides added ventilation to the driving compartment.

Fig. 8-8. The Marti car's overall custom design features obtain added elegance in addition to sportiness with the custom graphics/T-top combination.

Fig. 8-9. A custom touch to a custom T-top: glass-etched scrollwork.

Finally in Figs. 8-7, 8-8, and 8-9 are views of Charles Marti's "Bye Bye" Trans-Am. Old style Trans Ams were exceedingly popular for T-topping. Originally a stocker, a Cars & Concepts T-top assembly was added to give the car a sporty look. The T-tops in this instance fortify the "racy" look of the car, conceived along "Street Racer" lines.

Chapter 9

Decorative Sunroofs and T-tops

There are many ways to add to the decorative appeal of a sunroof or T-Top. It might be as simple as tinting the glass or adding striping, or as involved as etching the glass.

TINTING

Many of the T-tops and sunroofs produced today come in smoked and tinted glass versions or with built in sun grids. Occasionally you will come across some manufactured units that are clear glass units. Some folks may prefer the clear glass versions, but tinted glass has a lot more going for it. For one thing it helps minimize glare; for another it filters out the sun's rays which build up heat in a car, an unwanted factor inhibiting rider comfort.

If an existing sunroof or T-top does not contain tinted glass, there is no major problem. One can have sunroofs tinted the same way one has household windows tinted. Locate a good glass tinting shop that specializes in this service and bring the sunroof or removable glass sunroof segment to the local tinter. He will be able to apply standard stick-on window film for a minimal cost, usually not exceeding 15 dollars.

If you want to do the job yourself, you can buy window tint film in rolls from most national automotive aftermarket supply houses such as H. E. Rose, J. C. Whitney (mail order), Firestone, etc. You can also obtain window film from such sources as Sears, Montgomery Ward, K-Mart, J. C. Penney, etc.

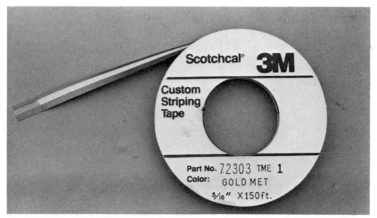

Fig. 9-1. 3M striping decor tape available in a wide variety of sizes and colors.

Window film is easy to apply for even the most casual do-it-yourselfer. First, the film is cut to size allowing a half inch or so overlap on each side. Then the protective backing is peeled off (if the brand chosen is this type). Next the glass section of the sunroof is thoroughly cleaned, preferably with a grease-removing solution such as Dupont Clesol or R-M Pre-Cleano. The glass (or film) is thoroughly wet down (check the instruction sheet provided with the film for exact requirements). The film is then applied onto the glass, and the excess water is squeezed off. Work from the center out, removing all water and air bubbles thoroughly.

A few drops of diswashing detergent will inhibit the film from adhering prematurely. Done properly, the film will permanently adhere to the glass. The final and simplest step is trimming the film down to the size of the glass, which is done with a razor glace or X-Acto knife.

STRIPING

A simple and inexpensive way to decorate an existing sunroof and T-top is with standard automotive striping tape. It is available at auto supply stores or automotive bodywork and paint supply outlets. Decor tapes are marketed in various widths of single, double, and even triple versions. The best striping tapes are the 1/16-inch or 1/8-inch versions. Wider tapes look hokey on sunroofs and sunroof frame corners.

On the sunroof in Fig. 9-2, we used a double line tape, 1/6-inch and 1/8-inch in parallel. The 3-M tape (Fig. 9-1) is the best for this particular application. 3-M tape comes with both a protective backing and a clear overlay tape. The backing is first removed and the tape lines are positioned and run along the chosen area (Fig. 9-2). Then the clear overlay tape is removed leaving tape stripes firmly affixed to the surface.

Figure 9-3 shows a Stretch Forming van sunroof visually enhanced by means of auto striping tape. This simple, inexpensive touch does much to improved the aesthetic aspects of the sunroof.

GLASS ETCHING

Glass etching in window decor is popular on cars today. Glass etching tends to individualize as well as decorate. Since sunroofs and T-tops are predominantly glass, this type of decorative approach is both desirable and welcome.

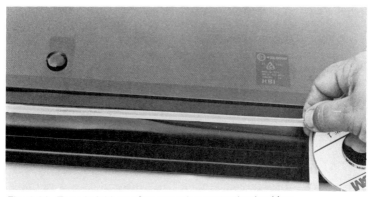

Fig. 9-2A. Tape is laid on after removing protective backing.

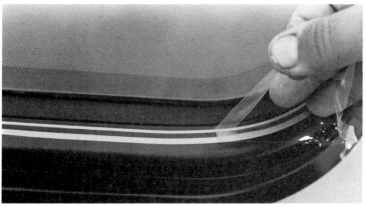

Fig. 9-2B. Covering is removed leaving stripes secured.

Fig. 9-3. Tape-striped sunroof.

Materials

Etching glass is not as hard as it appears. The only requirements are a good sandblaster and the proper masking medium. Sandblasters may be rented, and the masking rubber may be purchased from gravestone cutter supply sources or directly from the manufacturers.

The most necessary ingredient for glass sandblasting is sand mask stencil medium. This rubber-like, heavy stencil material is manufactured by Hartco Inc., a company based in Cincinnati, Ohio. Hartco Sand Mask Stencil (designated #100) was primarily developed for use in sandblasting wood, glass, and similar material where sandblasting times are not excessive or as prolonged as in blasting stone. Hartco #100 Sanding Stencil differs from other stenciling materials in many ways. It is durable, thick (.035 gauge), and has an adhesive side covered with a protective backing.

Figure 9-4 shows a roll of Hartco as it comes out of the box with its protective back coating. Before using this stencil medium, it is advised that the film be carefully checked since the material is easily affected by heat, which it may be subjected to in transit from manufacturer to consumer. Check to see that the material has not become stiff or brittle due to adverse heat or weather conditions. It should be soft and pliable. It must also be stored carefully since humidity, direct sunlight, and heat can have a detrimental effect on storage life.

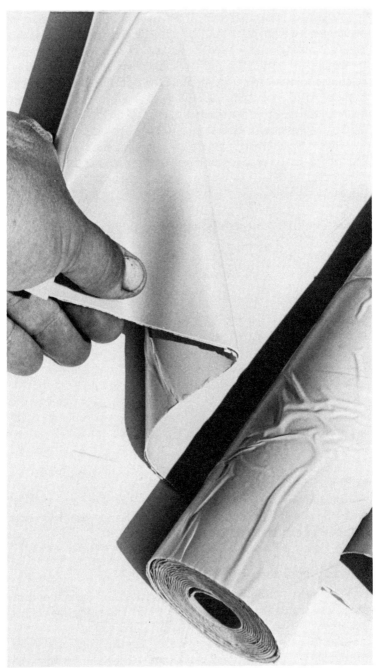

Fig. 9-4. Hartco Sand Mask medium is available in rolls and is self-adhesive.

Prior to utilizing this stencil in a glass blasting situation, it is recommended that you experiment with the materials. Try different pressure settings on the sandblaster and nozzle-to-stencil distance to obtain best results. Record workable characteristics for future reference. Check early test samples closely. If the stencil medium in the test run appears discolored due to excessive heat generated by overblasting, either the nozzle is being held too close to the stencil or the air pressure is excessive.

Hartco Sand Mask is marketed in various size rolls. The size required depends on the width of the glass section to be etched. As a guide, here are standard available sizes and their suggested prices:

Sand Mask 100-S Stencil Suggested Consumer Price List

Product Code	Roll size	Quantity	
		1-5	6-17
100-S-10	10 1/2″ × 10 yds.	21.14	20.08
100-S-12	12 3/4″ × 10 yds.	25.64	24.36
100-S-14	14 1/2″ × 10 yds.	29.21	27.75
*100-S-18	18 3/4″ × 10 yds.	37.69	35.81
100-S-25	25 ″ × 10 yds.	50.31	47.79
100-S-30	30 1/2″ × 10 yds.	61.39	58.32

*suggested material sizing for all sunroofs

Sand Mask 1005-18 stencil medium may be obtained from mortuary decorative supply sources.

Sand Mask is not cheap, but one roll will do about ten sunroofs or seven pairs of T-tops. The recommended Hartco size (which we utilized) for sunroofs and T-tops is the 100-S-18.

Masking Procedure

Thoroughly clean the glass piece to be etched to rid it of dirt, grease, or similar residue (Fig. 9-5). Now it is ready for stencil placement.

The first step is to cut an appropriate length of sand mask from the supply roll about 1/2 inch wider and 1/2 inch longer than the sunroof glass section to be etched. Peel away the protective stencil

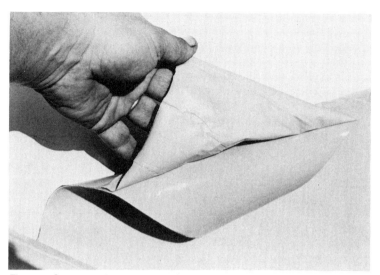

Fig. 9-5. Stencil backing is removed.

backing. Apply the sand mask by pressing it firmly onto the glass, working out any air bubbles as you go along. You may have to peel back the mask and re-apply it if bubbling persists; for best results, work from the center out. With the masking medium firmly applied, turn the sunroof over (Fig. 9-6). Trim away excess masking cutting close to the edge of the glass as shown in Fig. 9-7.

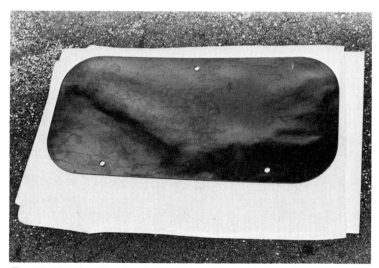

Fig. 9-6. After stencil medium is affixed, panel is turned over and excess overlap cut along the edge.

123

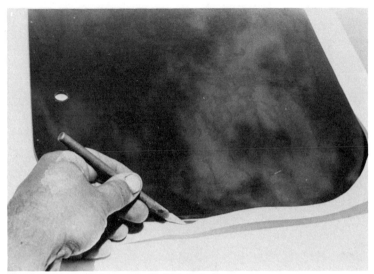

Fig. 9-7. Excess is trimmed with X-Acto knife.

Design a pattern for application on the glass, then work out a full-size pattern template drawing on a piece of posterboard or similar rigid paper material. Since the design shown here consists of two similar scrolls applied to each half section of the sunroof glass, we made one pattern which will be traced on one half then flipped to trace an identical scroll pattern on the opposite half of the glass.

Draw the scroll pattern on posterboard (Fig. 9-8) and cut it out

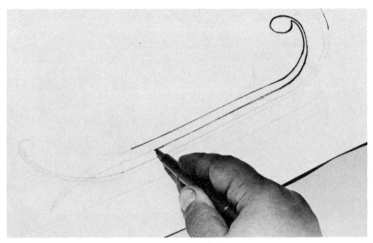

Fig. 9-8. Pattern is drawn on posterboard which will serve as design transfer stencil.

Fig. 9-9. Stencil (posterboard) is cut out.

(Fig. 9-9). Transfer the master half-side stencil to the Sand Mask already affixed to the sunroof glass (Fig. 9-10). An easy way to transfer the pattern is to spray paint through the stencil as it is held in place on the masking film (Fig. 9-11). First one side is sprayed, then the pattern stencil is flipped over to the second half and sprayed again. The two sides become a single symmetrical scroll pattern that matches exactly on both sides.

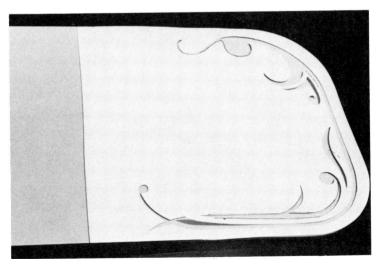

Fig. 9-10. Cutout is placed over one side of stencil mask on glass.

Fig. 9-11. After one side is sprayed, the poster stencil is flipped over to duplicated the pattern on the second half.

Now take an X-Acto knife with a pointed #11 blade and cut out the scrollwork pattern transferred to the sand mask material (Fig. 9-12). Peel away the pattern design sections, and you are ready to etch the pattern into the glass.

Etching the Glass

Take the sandblaster and hook it to an air power source, which

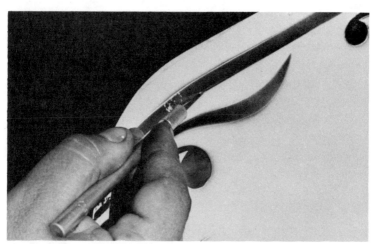

Fig. 9-12. Stencil medium affixed to glass is then cut and peeled.

in this case is a compressor of a least 2 horsepowers. Compressors and sandblasters may be rented, and you will need both.

Holding the sandblaster tip or sand exhaust nozzle about a foot away from the masked sunroof glass, depress the release lever. Move the blaster nozzle over the cut out portion of the mask in brisk, even, back-and-forth motions until you have achieved the degree or density of etching desired. Work the blaster only until you have rendered a discernable "etch" on the glass surface. Don't prolong the action until you wear deeply into the glass plate (Fig. 9-13). Once the sanded pattern is ingrained equal throughout, you can peel away the remaining sand mask to reveal the etched surface pattern (Fig. 9-14). Figure 9-15 shows the completed sunroof etching job.

T-top etching is handles the same way as sunroofs except that a larger area is rendered and masked. A design pattern is laid onto the T-top masking covering in the same manner as the sunroof, then peeled away (Fig. 9-16). The T-top is then blasted holding the nozzle further away than in the sunroof procedure so as to obtain a less radically etched surface with less of a surface-grain pattern (Fig. 9-17). The blasting unit used here is the Brut pressure blaster. It is one of the most efficient models available and ideally suited for refined glass etching as pressure and sand flow can be valve controlled in order to do exacting work. Figure 9-18 shows the T-top sporting a highly stylized etched scroll motif.

For those of you who have no access to sandblasting equipment

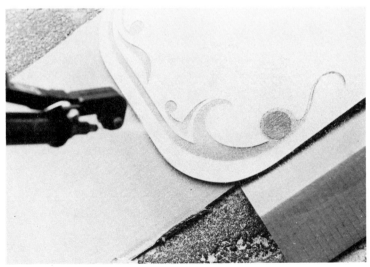

Fig. 9-13. Panel is sandblasted.

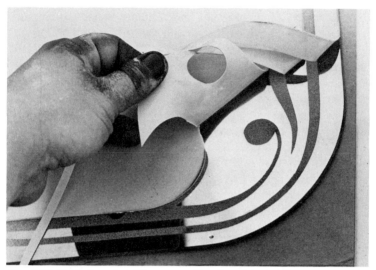

Fig. 9-14. Protective stencil is removed leaving etched pattern.

or equipment rental, there is an alternate route. You may carry the procedure up to the point of applying and cutting the stencil mask, then bring the sunroof(s) or T-tops to a local commercial sandblasting facility to have the job commercially done under your supervision and recommendations. A local sandblaster should be able to tackle the job for no more than $20 if he is fair and honest. All you have

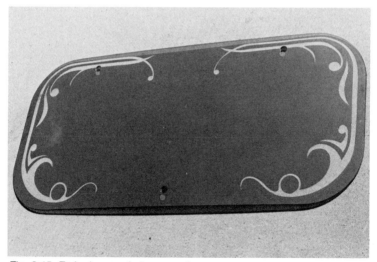

Fig. 9-15. Etched sunroof glass panel.

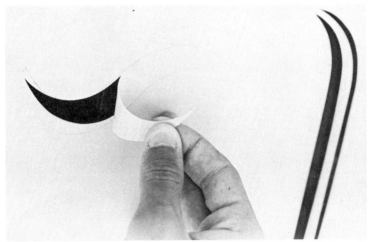

Fig. 9-16. Stencil for T-top is fashioned in manner similar to sunroofs.

to do is purchase, apply, and cut the sand masking material. If you cannot obtain the sand mask from local retail sandblasting accessory outlets (or gravestone suppliers), you may order it directly from:

Custom Coated Products
1280 Glendale-Milford Road
Cincinnati, OH
Phone: (513) 771-4430

Fig. 9-17. T-top is blasted.

129

Fig. 9-18. Etched T-top. T-top shown here is a Cars & Concepts unit.

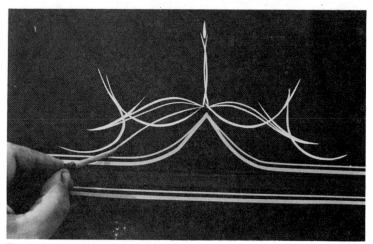

Fig. 9-19. Hand-striped design.

Fig. 9-20. Sunroof featuring both taped and hand-designed decor.

PINSTRIPING

Hand pinstriping is always an effective and attractive custom decorative approach (Fig. 9-19). It is not within the average decorator's realm, however, as pinstriping is an art that must be acquired with practice. You can engage the services of a local pinstriper who can do the job with minimal expenditure on your part. Figure 9-20 shows a trick pinstripe design integrated in a sunroof.

Chapter 10

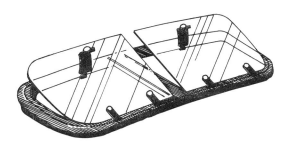

Maintenance

Except for the more complex and sophisticated electric sunroof models, sunroofs are fairly easy to maintain. Lubricating the hinges and securing mechanisms is necessary, as well as preventing leaks, rust, and corrosion.

REMOVING SUNROOFS

All sunroof glass panels today are removable for maintenance; some are easier to remove than others. The standard offerings on OEM cars lift out with a simple front clip(s) release of the glass panel which can then be swung back and removed as with the unit on the Nissan Pulsar illustrated in Fig. 10-1. The two back hinges remaining disengage by sliding the entire sunroof panel to the side allowing the hinge pins to telescope out of their respective retainers. Most OEM factory sunroofs come off in this manner.

Accessory sunroofs also disengage similarly; some have a more positive securing system. Figures 10-2, 10-3, and 10-4 show a typical sunroof panel release system such as in the Stretch Forming after-market sunroof. The same latch mechanism that opens and raises the sunroof panel can be disengaged by pulling out the two spring-loaded locking pins (Fig. 10-2). The glass panel is then pulled up but retained by the two quick-release clips on the side opposite the securing latch (Fig. 10-3). The two remaining clips can then be disengaged by pushing down as shown in Fig. 10-4.

Fig. 10-1. Standard OEM removal and maintenance is simple.

Fig. 10-2. Latch pin is pulled.

LUBRICATION AND RUST PREVENTION

Hinges and the simple working components of the sunroof should be kept oiled well to prevent binding and wearing away of chromed hinge pins and retainer tubes or shafts. The best oiling and lubricating medium for this purpose is WD-40, available at all hardware stores and similar outlets. WD-40 (Fig. 10-5) is a very ef-

Fig. 10-3. Panel is lifted.

Fig. 10-4. Catches are released.

Fig. 10-5. WD-40 lubricant.

Fig. 10-6. A spray concentrating tube comes with each can.

ficient penetrating oil that is thin enough to work into confined and close-fitting hinge mechanisms securing glass sunroof panels to their frames. WD-40 is unsurpassed for freeing sticky hinges, protecting and thoroughly coating metal (due to its highly penetrant property), loosening rusted hinges and shafts, and inhibiting metal-to-metal "squeaking." WD-40 combats corrosive elements, driving out

Fig. 10-7. Hinge retainers are sprayed.

Fig. 10-8. Pin and catch retainers are oiled.

moisture that may tend to build up in confined areas. To get into those confined areas, a small tube comes with each can that fits into the spray nozzle to pinpoint the oil spray when the pressure release lever on the can is depressed (Fig. 10-6).

Proper and effective lubrication procedure is as simple as soiling the hinge mechanisms on a Pulsar Factory sunroof. First, thoroughly oil and saturate the hinge shaft mechanism located on the car's sunroof frame (Fig. 10-7). Next liberally lubricate the pin retainer (the housing hole that the hinge pin slides into) on the inside. Concentrate the oil flow into the opening by using the narrow tube provided with WD-40 (Fig. 10-8). The swivel pin on the securing latch of the glass panel should also be oiled carefully (Fig. 10-9).

Fig. 10-9. Spray the release/opening latch too.

MAINTAINING T-TOPS

T-tops basically slip on and off when the retaining handle is opened; there are no internal working or hinging mechanisms involved. T-top frames should be kept clean at all times. Where chrome and stainless steel is involved, the fine polished metal finishes should be frequently treated with a good chrome or metal polish such as Noxon or Simichrome.

When T-tops are removed they are stored in the back seat or, more commonly, in the trunk of the vehicle. They should *always* be put into the protective covers (Fig. 10-10) provided with all T-tops, whether they are factory installed or accessory additive components.

Prevalent problems with T-tops are vehicle break-in and T-top theft, both of which are becoming very common. A thief with a coat hanger can slip by the window glass and disengage the T-top retaining handles giving him easy access to the car interior and the T-tops themselves, which are very saleable on the "midnight" sales market.

The Autosafe Corporation markets and accessory T-top lock that has solved this problem. It may be obtained from auto dealers and T-top outlets nationwide. The autosafe lock mechanisms fit over the T-top's release handles and can be key locked (Fig. 10-11). The AS 500 model fits all 1968-1982 Corvette, Hurst, and American T-tops. Made of chrome-plated die-cast steel, the Autosafe T-top locks also

Fig. 10-10. Covers should always be used when T-top panels are removed or stored in trunk.

Fig. 10-11. T-top release handle locks are highly recommended.

offer a matching Corvette insignia option available for the earliest model Corvettes. An Autosafe Model AS 400 (GM) version is also available to fit all 1978-1982 Firebird, Camaro, Grand Prix, Cutlass, Regal, and Monte Carlo models with factory or dealer installed T-tops.

ELECTRIC SUNROOFS

Because electric sunroofs are more complex and contain numerous working parts, they should be serviced and maintained regularly. The motor mechanisms should be checked and, if necessary, adjusted, lubricated, etc. A once-a-year check by an authorized dealer (or installer) is advised in order to keep the electric sunroof in tip-top working condition. Table 10-1 (courtesy Hollandia) gives some service information of interest to Hollandia and similar electric sunroof owners.

Occasionally, due to auto accidents, owner carelessness etc., the sunroof panels may be damaged or broken. Replacement glass may be obtained from the original sunroof or T-top source. In the event that the dealer does not stock T-top replacement parts, they may be readily obtained from Central Service Co., St. Louis, Missouri. Central has an extensive inventory of T-top parts and replacement glass for Fisher (OEM), Cars & Concepts, Hurst, Corvette, and Datsun 28OZ (OEM). Central Service can be reached by phone. Their number: (314) 531-7017.

When in need of replacement parts, always check the source or manufacturer of the particular sunroof, Fig. 10-12. They all carry an extensive spare parts inventory.

Table 10-1. Hollandia Electric Sunroof Maintenance.

SERVICE INFORMATION.

1. MAINTENANCE.

    1. The rails on each side of the roof opening must be kept clean.
    2. Check the four draintubes regularly to be sure that they are not
       plugged with dirt or leaves.
       If plugged, clean tubes with a flexible wire or an air hose.
    3. Treat the vinyl top regularly with a suitable vinyl protecting
       liquid.

2. ADJUSTMENTS.

    Panel alignment may be needed if panel does not fit perfectly into the
    roof opening.
    Rear corners of panel should rise even with car roof when panel is fully
    closed. If not, this can be adjusted by loosening the front panel screws,
    moving front edge of panel up or down as needed and refastening the screws.

3. DIAGNOSIS AND REPAIR.

Complaint	Possible cause	Repair
1. Water is not draining properly from roof housing	1. Draintube(s) plugged or restricted with dirt	Clean tubes with flexible wire or air hose
	2. Twist in draintube	Reinstall draintube
2. Water is dripping from headlining	1. Draintube(s) disconnected from nipple(s)	Apply cement on nipple and insert draintube(s).
	2. Draintube(s) have a leak.	Install new drain tube
3. Rattling	1. Loosened part(s) on sliding panel or headlining frame	Tighten up.
	2. Torsion spring(s) have been installed beneath instead of above torsion plate on sliding panel	Reinstall sliding panel correctly.
4. Windnoise when panel is closed	1. Edges of panel are not flush and even with the car roof	Adjust panel height

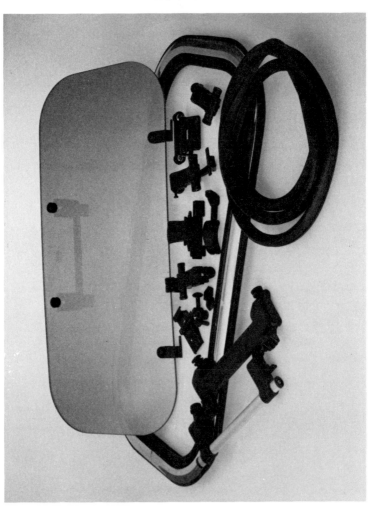

Fig. 10-12. C.R. Laurence offers an excellent spare parts replacement program for hard-to-find sunroof parts. Courtesy C.R. Laurence.

Index

Edited by Steven Bolt

OTHER POPULAR TAB BOOKS OF INTEREST

TAB   TAB BOOKS Inc.

Blue Ridge Summit, Pa. 17214

Send for FREE TAB Catalog describing over 750 current titles in print.